Skilling India

Skilling India

Challenges and Opportunities

S. Nayana Tara
N. S. Sanath Kumar

BEP BUSINESS EXPERT PRESS

First published in 2018 by
Business Expert Press, LLC
222 East 46th Street, New York, NY 10017
www.businessexpertpress.com

ISBN-13: 978-1-94784-333-2 (paperback)
ISBN-13: 978-1-94784-334-9 (e-book)

Business Expert Press Human Resource Management and Organizational Behavior Collection

Collection ISSN: 1946-5637 (print)
Collection ISSN: 1946-5645 (electronic)

Cover and interior design by S4Carlisle Publishing Services Private Ltd., Chennai, India

First edition: 2018

10 9 8 7 6 5 4 3 2 1

Printed in the United States of America.

Abstract

India's transition to a knowledge-based economy requires a new generation of educated and skilled people. Its competitive edge will be determined by its people's ability to create, share, and use knowledge effectively. A knowledge economy requires India to develop workers—knowledge workers and knowledge technologists—who are flexible and analytical and can be the driving force for innovation and growth. Developing skilled workers enhances the efficiency and flexibility of the labor market; skills bottlenecks are reduced, skilled workers are more easily absorbed into the economy, and their job mobility is improved. In this light, an effort is made in this book to describe and analyze governmental skill development initiatives in India. The book focuses on the status of vocational education programs, challenges of achieving quality and attaining competitive excellence in a globalized socioeconomic order, and the role of government and industry in achieving these avowed goals. The book also dwells on the need to revive traditional family-centric vocations pursued in the rural communities, especially those dying village-based vocations that provide livelihood options to a multitude of socially disadvantaged artisans, and integrate them into the fabric of skill development initiatives in place.

The book provides a systematic understanding of the processes of skill formation and provides several pathways for enhancing entrepreneurial skills in a business ecosystem with a huge knowledge capital gained through skill development initiatives. Toward this end, the book seeks to contribute toward understanding the structures and processes of governance and initiatives for enhancing the quality of skilling programs. The book also dwells on various opportunities and challenges of augmenting a multitude of skilled workforces made available through various skilling initiatives and programs.

Keywords

governance, Indian National Skill Development Policy, skill development challenges, skilling opportunities, vocational education and training

Contents

Acknowledgements

We are grateful to Prof. Matthais Pilz, University of Cologne, Germany, for his constant support and sharing his views on Indian skill development scene. We also wish to acknowledge Dr. V. Mohan Kumar, Chief Functionary, Indian Adult Education Association, for his thoughtful insights.

CHAPTER 1

Introduction

Skill Development: A Global Scene

The past three decades have witnessed dramatic changes in labor force participation in the global economy. This commenced with a dramatic shock in the 1990s, when the entry of the People's Republic of China (PRC), India, and the former Soviet Union into the global economy, contributing 1.47 billion workers, effectively doubled the size of the global pool of labor and depressed wages (particularly for low-skilled labor) globally. More recently, however, Asia in particular has transitioned to a trend of wage escalation alongside shortages of certain types of skills (Sungsup Ra et al. 2015).

The doubling of the size of the global pool of labor in the 1990s resulted in an explosion in the number of workers, thereby shifting the global balance of power to capital and reducing the ratio of capital to labor in the world economy to 61 percent of what it would have been had the PRC, India, and the former Soviet Union not joined the world economy (Freeman 2006). More specifically, the massive influx of workers from these countries, more so the PRC and India, injected a huge pool of similar skilled workers with wages only around one-fourth of other developing countries such as Mexico or South Africa. This enabled the PRC and India to capture global production jobs while forcing many developing and developed countries to rethink their growth strategy to produce more value-added products to survive in the new global economy (Freeman 2006).

Although primary education is nearing universalization in much of Asia, attainment of secondary (particularly upper-secondary) education and postsecondary Technical and Vocational Education and Training (TVET) and higher education remains much lower, particularly in developing countries in Asia. The net enrollment rate for primary education in Asia as a whole was more than 90 percent in 2011 (UNESCO and UNICEF 2013), dropping to 64.1 percent for secondary education (UNDESA 2012b). It is also noteworthy that although many upper-secondary graduates directly enter the labor market, relatively small shares of upper-secondary-level students in Asia are enrolled in TVET programs, with the share exceeding 25 percent only in the PRC, Indonesia, and Thailand (Ra et al. 2015).

Relatively low rates of access to various types of TVET have important implications for economic competitiveness and skills mismatches. A 2013 ILO survey of ASEAN Employers on Skills and Competitiveness identified the lack of vocational training as the second greatest source of skills gaps (Emerging Markets Consulting 2014). Institution-based TVET in many Asian countries does not have the capacity to meet the training needs even of new entrants to the labor market. For example, while there are about 13 million entrants into the labor market every year in India, the current capacity of the country's training system can train only 25 percent of them (Panth 2013). This low capacity is partially due to low public spending on TVET, for example, less than 5 percent of the education budget in South Asia (Panth 2013). At the same time, firms are not picking up the shortfall. In many Asian countries, employers provide very limited on-the-job training to employees. This tends to be particularly true in economies where small and medium-sized enterprises and informal sector jobs account for a large share of employment.

Skills mismatch in India is evidenced by the fact that (i) India has consistently ranked among the top three countries in the region in terms of firms' difficulty in filling vacancies since 2011, with 58 percent of the employers surveyed reporting difficulty in finding people with the requisite skills in 2015, and (ii) India has pervasive unemployment and underemployment among youth, even among university graduates, with one in three graduates up to the age of 29 being unemployed. This is consistent with the findings by the World Bank enterprise surveys that suggest many young people, even those with university degrees, are unemployable because of a lack of technical and vocational skills needed by employers (World Bank 2013).

Worryingly, skills mismatch in Asia is not just about inadequate education; it is also about the education systems' failure to keep up with the evolving needs of the labor market and specific skilling needs. In terms of occupation-specific skills, skills shortages in Asia vary between economies and sub-regions, and key occupations facing skills shortages include engineers, technicians, sales representatives, managers, accountants, information technology staff, and workers in skilled trades (APEC 2013).

Across South Asia, skills development is a common concern. In India, for example, the government launched a sweeping reform targeting skills training for 400 million workers by 2022. For Sri Lanka, building job-relevant skills is a pivotal step toward building a more competitive and efficient middle-income economy. Healthy economic growth and structural changes in the economy have been driving increased demand for skilled labor in Sri Lanka. However, the skills gap that has emerged with the changing labor market conditions may be starting to hold back the economy (Dhar 2016)

Similar sentiments are expressed in another thought-provoking study of employment and skills strategies in South East Asia (Martinez-Fernandez and Powell 2009)

The study highlights the following challenges of skills formation in ASEAN region:

- The links between urbanization, demographic changes, and investments in skills and employment needs more attention
- Lack of decent and productive employment
- Need to reform labor market institutions
- Skills mismatch is evident
- Poverty reduction still challenges development in the region
- Growth of the informal economy is not slowing down
- Migration and mobility represent both challenges and opportunities
- Impact of Free Trade Agreements (FTAs) remains largely unexplored
- Industrial composition is fragmented
- Lack of entrepreneurial development linked to productive activities

While skill formation of high quality in countries of South Asia and other regions faces several challenges and roadblocks, it would be interesting to know how skill development as a concept and program is viewed by various countries. We present a brief profile of skill development models/programs implemented in some selected countries.

International Models in Skill Development

We present as follows some of the international models of skill development initiatives that are in vogue.

Australia

The Australian Qualifications Framework (AQF) is a quality-assured national framework of qualifications in the school, vocational education and training (VET), and higher education sectors in Australia. The AQF comprises:

A) National guidelines for each of the current national qualifications issued in the senior secondary school, vocational education and training, and higher education sectors

B) Policies and guidelines for articulation, credit transfer, and recognition of prior learning register of authorities empowered by governments to accredit qualifications

C) Register of institutions authorized to issue qualifications

D) Protocols for issuing qualifications, and

E) A governance structure for monitoring the implementation of the AQF and for advising ministers, including recommendations for change.

F) Some of the key features of the AQF are:
   I. Recognition of prior learning
   II. Seamless pathways (for enabling easy movement into and out of vocational training)
   III. Credit transfer.

Germany

VET is regarded as the pillar of the educational system in Germany. Two-thirds of young people undergo vocational training in the dual system. This training would ideally last two to three-and-a-half years, depending on one's occupation. It is described as a "dual system" as training is carried out in two places of learning: at the workplace and in a vocational school. The aim of training in the dual system is to provide a broad-based basic to advanced vocational training and impart the skills and knowledge necessary to practice a skilled occupation within a structured course of training. Those completing the training are entitled to undertake skilled work in one of about 355 recognized occupations requiring formal training. The only requisite is that the student should have completed full-time schooling before commencing vocational training. The key success factor for the German system is the added focus on apprenticeship.

United Kingdom

The National Vocational Qualifications (NVQs) were created in response for the felt need for qualifications to be made flexible but rigorous and nationally recognized. NVQs are also part of "Modern Apprenticeships" that are funded through work-based learning. The funding varies between occupational sectors and by age group. The national framework covers general secondary and tertiary education, VET, work-based learning, and prior learning. Accreditation of Prior Experiential Learning (APEL) describes the process of giving formal recognition to learning that derives from personal experiences often gained in employment or voluntary work situations. At the industry level, Sector Skills Councils (SSCs) have been licensed and social partners are also engaged. SSCs are tasked with drawing up occupational standards for their sector that will feed into the national reform of qualifications. The government expects each SSC to draw up a Sector Skills Agreement, in which employers and unions identify skills and productivity needs in their sector and the necessary actions to meet those needs.

Singapore

The National Skills Recognition System (NSRS) is Singapore's national framework for establishing work performance standards, identifying job competencies and certifying skills acquisition. It is implemented by the Standards, Productivity, and Innovation Board with the support of the Ministry of Manpower and the Ministry of Trade and Industry. This has helped the industry train skills-standards consultants and assessors, as well as to develop On-Job-Training (OJT) blueprints for the skills-standards established. To assess the workers, assessment centers were set up. Workers can be certified at centralized assessment centers, workplace, or a combination of both. Supporting the NSRS implementation framework are promotional activities and financial incentives for the industries. NSRS is promoted at four levels, that is, national, industry, company, and workforce, in collaboration with employer groups, industry associations, economic agencies, and unions. All this is illustrative of some of the major frameworks available internationally for driving policy in skill development.

United States of America

In the American system, general high schools keep all students in the same school till the end of secondary level irrespective of their aptitudes and add vocational programs to the academic curriculum differentiating their learning paths. According to Gasskov (2000), more than 60 percent of high school students in the United States enroll in at least one vocational subject. Variants of this system are in vogue in other countries like Sweden and the United Kingdom.

France

The French system consists of separate vocational and technical schools along with general education schools separating the students in the lower classes into the two streams depending on their aptitudes. The "dual system" operating in Germany combines training in industry with part-time instruction in vocational schools and is promoted by employers. Again, different countries have opted for variants of vocational education and training systems involving combinations of these three systems.

While the foregoing classification of vocational education is on the basis of institutional arrangements and content, *The World Employment Report*, 1998–1999 (ILO 1999) distinguishes between three major types of training systems operating in different countries using a classification based on the inter se responsibilities of the social partners and the impetus for training. These are (a) cooperative, (b) enterprise-based, and (c) state-driven systems. Other classifications based on source of financing that funds vocational education are also possible.

China

In China, the Law on Vocational Education was adopted in 1996 with a goal to have equal number of students in vocational and academic secondary schools. Vocational education is offered in lower and upper middle schools with lower middle schools largely in the rural areas. There are three types of upper-middle vocational schools: (i) specialized secondary schools, (ii) skilled workers school, and (iii) vocational high schools. In 2007, there were 14,832 upper-middle vocational schools with an enrollment of 19.87 million students. As compared to this, in India, 380,000 students in classes XI and XII were enrolled in schools under vocational education in 2005 to 2006. In China, tertiary VE is also offered in vocational colleges for students enrolling from general and vocational middle schools, thus enabling vertical mobility. The VE was earlier considered a dead-end. China addressed this problem by starting key schools offering better quality facilities and pathways for progressing beyond secondary education. However, in China, fees paid by the students of public vocational secondary schools are among the highest in the world (ADB 2006). In addition, there coexist some student support schemes that either provide free boarding and lodging to needy students or waive their tuition fees. The Vocational Education Law in China mandates that enterprises spend 1.5 percent of the workers' total annual salary on training. In additions, the country promotes partnership between schools and enterprises. Efforts are made by schools to be engaged in partnership with enterprises for mobilizing private resources for training and improve the match between the demand for and supply of skills. The partnership between schools and enterprises provides apprenticeship and internship opportunities for trainees.

Botswana

A well-known example of combining training with income-generating activities is the *Botswana brigades*. Brigades are community-based independent development organizations involved in providing training, employment opportunities, and services to the local community. Brigades offer commercial services to the communities, such as auto repair, general mechanics, plumbing, construction, and electricity. Horticulture and so on run workshops and participate in public tenders (e.g., construction). It is assumed that the production activities of the brigades recover at least 20 percent of the recurrent training cost.

In countries with large vocational education systems, there is a trend toward increasing generalization of the vocational curricula to make the system nonterminal. In New Zealand, for example, the first step toward this end was to make 13 years of education (general and basic education, including 1 year of preschool) compulsory for the entire population. Similarly, in Korea, streaming into vocational education was delayed till high school (for 3 years after grade 11; Tara and Kumar n.d.).

Skill development as a formal program in India is relatively new, though technical education has a long history. Recognizing the importance of equipping a huge multitude of workforce to acquire quality skills in a rapidly "globalized" India is a major milestone in the saga of Indian national development. The recent establishment of an exclusive Ministry of Skill Development by the government is a pointer to the fact that Indian workforce needs quality training to compete in an international milieu where professional excellence is a key factor. In the next section we discuss various initiatives taken in skill development in India.

Skill Development in India

India is expected to become one of the most populous nations by 2025, with a headcount of around 1.4 billion. The country's population pyramid is expected to "bulge" across the 15 to 64 years age bracket over the next decade, increasing the working-age population from approximately 761 million to 869 million during 2011 to 2020. Consequently, until 2020, India will be experiencing a period of "demographic bonus," where the growth rate of the working-age population would exceed that of the total population (*Population Projection and Its Socio-Economic Implications in India: A State Level Projection Till 2020*, International Institute for Population Sciences).

India is poised to become the world's youngest country by 2020, with an average age of 295 years, and account for around 28 percent of the world's workforce. In comparison, during the same period, the average age is expected to be 37 years in China and the United States and 45 years in Western Europe, while China's demographic dividend would start tapering off. An increasing proportion of working population will provide a window of opportunity to improve labor productivity, increase domestic production, enhance revenue from services, increase savings, and reduce the burden of old residents on the working population. Empowered with unique demographic advantages and guided efforts, India is poised to position itself among developed economies within the next 10 to 15 years (Chenoy 2012).

In the Indian context, while concerted efforts in skill development has brought about a paradigm shift in addressing the issues of relevance in skill development, the gaps in skill development are to be identified to achieve the objectives of quantity, quality, outreach, and mobility while building on the foundation. Current studies indicate that net enrolment in vocational courses in India is about 5.5 million per year compared to 90 million in China and 11.3 million in the United States. A mere 2 percent of Indian workers are formally skilled. According to the 12th 5 Year Plan document, some major areas that merit attention are as follows: (a) the challenge of reaching out to the nonformal sector; (b) putting in place a National Skills Qualification Framework that lays down different levels of skills required by industry, which allows multiple points of entry and exit, recognizes prior learning, and allows for mobility across different levels; (c) putting in place a permanent institutional framework, entrusted with the requisite authority and resources and is responsible solely for skill development in the country; and (d) supporting students with soft-terms bank loans that are linked to their placement.

Recognizing the critical importance of skilling India, an exclusive Ministry of Skill Development and Entrepreneurship was established by the Government of India during 2015. The new ministry has put in place a National Policy for Skill Development and Entrepreneurship in

2015. The primary objective of this policy is to meet the challenge of skilling on a larger scale with speed, standard (quality) and sustainability. Skills development is the shared responsibility of the key stakeholders—government; the entire spectrum of corporate sector, community-based organizations, and outstanding, highly qualified and dedicated individuals who have been working in the skilling and entrepreneurship space for many years; and industry, trade organizations, and other stakeholders. The policy links skills development to improved employability and productivity in paving the way forward for inclusive growth in the country.

The magnitude of the task of skilling in India can be gauged by the following scenario (Mehrotra et al. 2012):

- 12.8 million annually entering the labor market for the first time
- 72.88 million employed in the organized sector
- 387.34 million working in the unorganized sector

Most of the formal skills-related training in the government apparatus happens through the Industrial Training Institutes (ITIs) and the Industrial Training Centres (ITCs), polytechnics and so on, which come under the Ministry of Labour and Employment. Many of these institutions have now been brought under the public-private partnership model. Informal skills-related training, including in traditional arts and crafts pursued in Indian villages, is also supported through different government ministries and skill development missions at the state level.

The vocational education system in the country faces the daunting task of achieving the goals of National Skill Development and Entrepreneurship policy of 2015. Foremost, the vocational education stream itself has poor visibility due to several reasons like low awareness among stakeholders and lack of parity in wage structure between formally qualified and vocationally trained graduates. Furthermore, public perception on skilling, which is viewed as the last option meant for those who have not been able to progress/opted out of the formal academic system, creates a low demand for vocational education. This is due mainly to the tendency of industry to discriminate skilled and unskilled persons, thereby depriving the skilled workforce of any meaningful economic incentive. This is also compounded by the fact that most of the vocational training programs are not aligned to the requirements of the industry.

Historical Milestones of Vocational Education in India

Education in India was generally identified with liberal education. The Education Dispatch, issued by Sir Charles Wood, the president of the Board of Control, famously known as Wood's Dispatch, formed the basis of the education policy of East India Company's government in India since 1854. Among others, the Dispatch, highlighted for the first time, the need for the introduction of occupational education for a sizeable segment of the student population. Furthermore, the Dispatch highlighted the need for imparting Western knowledge and information, to create a class of public servants, and to develop practical and vocational skills of the Indian people so that more and more articles could be produced and also to create a good market for consumption of those goods by the Indian population (http://www.vkmaheshwari.com/WP/?p=1389). Since then, several commissions, including the Hunter Commission (1882), the Hartog Committee (1929), and Sapru Committee (1934) among others, emphasized the vital role of vocational education in the country's economic development. The Hartog Committee recommended diversified courses in the schools to enable the students to prepare for industrial and commercial careers at the end of middle-school stage, as preparation for special instruction in technical and industrial schools. The Sapru Committee recommended 11 years of school education (5 years for primary, 3 for lower secondary, and 3 for higher secondary) with vocational studies commencing after 11 years of education. The main purpose of the Sapru Committee was to find ways and means of solving unemployment problems through diversified courses at the secondary stage. Nevertheless, it made little impact on the educational administration. It was the Wood–Abbot Commission (1936) that prompted the creation of a network of polytechnics in the country. The duration of polytechnic courses was 2 or 3 years depending on the courses offered in such institutions. These courses were offered in engineering or technical schools.

Prevocational Education

Skill development initiatives at the primary and upper-primary level in India are yet to fully take off in an organized manner. The importance of providing basic education along with introducing young people to vocational skills was recognized during preindependent India, mooted by the Father of the Nation, Mahatma Gandhi and holds a unique place in the history of elementary education in India. *The Selected Works of Gandhi* in six volumes (Navajivan Publishing House 1968) provides the Gandhian approach and philosophy of education highlighting the need for achieving high moral values, dignity of labor, and the importance of learning crafts at the early stages of education. The Wardha Commission of 1937 gave a concrete shape to this educational philosophy that would in essence provide children with education in reading, writing, and arithmetic in addition to teaching them a vocational skill, thereby inculcating in children the significance of dignity of labor. This is further reinforced by the observation of the Committee of Members of Parliament on National Policy on Education in 1967, which mentioned that work experience should be an integral part of general education at the school stage. This thought had been clearly enunciated by Gandhi's pedagogy of *Nai Talim* (the "new exercise") in 1937:

> Traditional and colonial forms of education had emphasized literacy and abstract, text-based knowledge which had been the domain of the upper castes. Gandhi's proposal to make handicrafts the centre of his pedagogy had as its aim to bring about a 'radical restructuring of the sociology of school knowledge in India' in which the 'literacies' of the lower castes—'such as spinning, weaving, leatherwork, pottery, metal-work, basket-making and book-binding'—would be made central. (Sykes 1988)

The major weakness of the present education system is the dysfunctional linkage between education and the world of work. It must be mentioned that preparation for the world of work must begin at an early stage of child's educational journey. The preparatory knowledge acquired at this stage would be the stepping stone for gaining advanced skill education at secondary and higher levels. It is a paradox that acquisition of skill at the primary and upper primary levels, which was propounded as an important part of the educational policy through such efforts as the Wardha Commission, promotion of Gandhi's pedagogy of *Nai Talim,* among others, the deluge of the Western educational philosophy, and the priority placed on rapid industrialization as the avowed need of the hour struck a major blow to prevocational education in India and its impact is felt even today. Perhaps the thoughts of Gandhi on the philosophy of education are best borne out by this comment:

> By education I mean an all-round drawing out of the best in child and man . . . body, mind and spirit. Literacy is not the end of education nor even the beginning. It is only one of the means by which man and woman can be educated. Literacy in itself is no education. I would therefore begin the child's education by teaching it a useful handicraft and enabling it to produce from the moment it begins its training. (Gandhi and Harijan 1937)

Following India's independence from Britain in 1947, the Radhakrishnan Commission (1948) recommended that in order to direct school students to vocational training at the end of class X, or school-leaving level, a large number of intermediate colleges should be opened. It said,

> The aim of these colleges would be to meet a variety of needs of our young men and women by giving a vocational bias to their courses by retaining at the same time their value in a system of general education as preparation for university courses. (Nayak and Rao 2008)

The Mudaliar Commission (1952) reiterated,

> the secondary education is a complete unit by itself and not merely a preparatory stage that at the end of this period the student should be in a position, if he wishes, to enter into responsibilities of life and take up some vocations. (Nayak and Rao 2008)

It also recommended diversification of the courses at the secondary stage. This resulted in the creation of multipurpose schools. During the First Five Year Plan period (1951–1956) about 250 multipurpose schools were established; during the Second Plan period the number of multipurpose schools was to be increased to 1,187. Unfortunately, for various reasons, including lack of proper appreciation of the scheme, inadequate preparation in terms of infrastructure and teaching staff, and overemphasis on preparation for university courses, the multipurpose schools were reduced to shadows of what they were originally intended to be. In 1955, the All India Council of Technical Education (AICTE) was set up to advice the Union Government on all aspects of technical education at the diploma as well as degree levels. It was about the same time that a network of Industrial Training Institutes to train the base-level industrial workers was created.

Some basic academic considerations again compelled the government to appoint the Education Commission of 1964 under the Chairmanship of Dr. D.S. Kothari to reexamine the entire educational system of the country keeping in view the national goal—improvement of quality and standard of education. The Kothari Commission suggested that at the higher-secondary stage there needed to be two distinctive streams: one, preparing students for advanced education in the universities and the professional colleges, and two, preparing students for a variety of occupations immediately after their completing the vocational studies to enter the labor market. In keeping with this recommendation, the commission suggested that for college-preparatory general education courses the duration may be 2 years and the duration of studies and training for the vocational stream may range from 1 to 3 years or more. Given the proper planning, cooperation, coordination, and implementation of the scheme, the commission felt it should be possible to divert at least 50 percent of the students who successfully completed 10 years of education to the vocational stream, thus reducing the pressure on the universities on one hand and preparing students for employment, including self-employment, on the other. For a majority of vocational higher-secondary students, it would be a terminal stage in a sense although further educational facilities should be made available on a large scale so that those in jobs may benefit through part-time or evening studies.

Conforming to these recommendations, the National Policy of Education Resolution (1968) stated that:

> There is need to increase facilities for technical and vocational education at secondary stage. Provisions of facilities for secondary and vocational education should conform particularly to requirements of the developing economy and real employment opportunities. Such linkage is necessary to make technical and

vocational education at the secondary stage effectively terminal. The facilities for technical and vocational education should be suitably diversified to cover a large number of fields such as agriculture, industry, trade and commerce, medicine and public health, home management, arts and crafts and secretarial training. (http://mhrd.gov.in/sites/upload_files/mhrd/files/document-reports/NPE-1968.pdf)

CHAPTER 2

Governmental Efforts to Promote Skill Development

Policy Approach for Skill Development and Vocational Education and Training

Although vocational education was recognized as an important ingredient for economic and social advancement, there had been no clear articulation of an exclusive policy on vocational education. However, this lacuna was addressed by the 12th Five Year Plan document (Government of India, Planning Commission 2013) that clearly states that there is an urgent need to mainstream skill formation in the formal education system. This was later evolved into a well-crafted policy on Skill Development and Entrepreneurship by the Government of India in 2015. The newly evolved National Policy for Skill Development and Entrepreneurship (2015) has the avowed goal of meeting the challenge of skilling at scale with speed, standard (quality), and sustainability. It aims to provide an umbrella framework to all skilling activities being carried out within the country, to align them to common standards and link skilling with demand centers. Given this, the policy has spelt out in greater detail about the ways and means of accomplishing these goals.

The core objective of the policy is to empower the individual, by enabling them to realize their full potential through a process of lifelong learning where competencies are accumulated via instruments such as credible certifications, credit accumulation, and transfer. As individuals grow, the society and nation also benefit from their productivity and growth. This will involve

1. making quality vocational training aspirational for both youth and employers whereby youth sees it as a matter of choice and employer acknowledges the productivity linked to skilled workforce by paying the requisite premium.

2. ensuring both vertical and horizontal pathways to skilled workforce for further growth by providing seamless integration of skill training with formal education.

3. focusing on an outcome-based approach toward quality skilling that on one hand results in increased employability and better livelihoods for individuals, and on the other, translates into improved productivity across primary, secondary, and tertiary sectors.

4. increasing the capacity and quality of training infrastructure and trainers to ensure equitable and easy access to every citizen.

5. addressing human resource needs by aligning supply of skilled workers with sectoral requirements of industry and the country's strategic priorities, including flagship programs like Make in India.

6. establishing an IT-based information system for aggregating demand and supply of skilled workforce that can help in matching and connecting supply with demand.

7. promoting national standards in the skilling space through active involvement of employers in setting occupational standards, helping develop curriculum, providing apprenticeship opportunities, participating in assessments, and providing gainful employment to skilled workforce with adequate compensation.

The core objective of the entrepreneurship framework is to coordinate and strengthen factors essential for growth of entrepreneurship across the country. This would include

- promoting entrepreneurship culture and make it aspirational.
- encouraging entrepreneurship as a viable career option through advocacy.
- enhancing support for potential entrepreneurs through mentorship and networks.
- integrating entrepreneurship education in the formal education system.
- fostering innovation-driven and social entrepreneurship to address the needs of the population at the bottom of the pyramid.

- ensuring ease of doing business by reducing entry and exit barriers.
- facilitating access to finance through credit and market linkages.
- promoting entrepreneurship among women.
- broadening the base of entrepreneurial supply by meeting specific needs of both socially and geographically disadvantaged sections of the society, including SCs, STs, OBCs, minorities, differently abled persons.

In order to accomplish these objectives, the policy enunciates a set of paradigms and enablers that form the driving principles of skill development and entrepreneurship in the country. These include (a) aspiration and advocacy, (b) capacity, (c) quality, (d) synergy, (e) mobilization and engagement, (f) global partnerships, (g) outreach, (h) ICT enablement, (i) trainers and assessors, (j) inclusivity, and (k) promotion of skilling among women.

The entrepreneurship policy framework proposes a nine-part entrepreneurship strategy:

A) Educate and equip potential and early-stage entrepreneurs across India.
B) Connect entrepreneurs to peers, mentors, and incubators.
C) Support entrepreneurs through Entrepreneurship Hubs (E-Hubs).
D) Catalyze a culture shift to encourage entrepreneurship.
E) Encourage entrepreneurship among underrepresented groups.
F) Promote entrepreneurship among women.
G) Improve ease of doing business.
H) Improve access to finance.
I) Foster social entrepreneurship and grassroots innovations.

Policy Framework for Skill Development

The policy framework has been developed to accomplish the vision of Skill India by adhering to the stated objectives. The framework outlines 11 major paradigms and enablers to achieve these objectives:

1. *Aspiration and advocacy*
2. *Capacity*

3. *Quality*
4. *Synergy*
5. *Mobilization and engagement*
6. *Global partnerships*
7. *Outreach*
8. *ICT enablement*
9. *Trainers and assessors*
10. *Inclusivity*
11. *Promotion of skilling among women.*

Aspiration and Advocacy

The need of the hour is to make skill development aspirational for boys and girls in our country. For skill training to be looked at as a matter of choice, it must (a) provide vertical growth pathways on the lines of the general education system, so that skill education and training is also seen as a valid route to earn degrees and diplomas and, consequently, to positions of authority linked to such qualifications; (b) be associated with growth and sustainable livelihood pathways; and (c) have a causal relationship with increased income for skilled workforce.

A) A national campaign will be launched within 3 months to create awareness and a positive pro-skilling environment. Communication packages and kits will be standardized to ensure quality and made available in all local languages with focused promotion through skill ambassadors, including eminent personalities. State-wise camps will be organized for skills awareness and mobilization. Social media will be effectively used to amplify the campaign and build publicity. A TV channel and a national community radio frequency dedicated to skilling will be promoted to enable communication and dissemination of information and opportunities relating to skills on a regular basis. The Skill India logo will also be used to promote the value of a skilled workforce and create momentum for skilling among the youth.

B) National skills universities and institutes will be promoted in partnership with states as centers of excellence for skill development and training of trainers, either as de novo institutions or as a part of existing university landscape. It is desired that these institutions become as aspirational for candidates as other premier institutes around the country. These institutions, apart from skilling candidates through affiliates and training the trainers, will also conduct extensive research to enhance the quality and delivery of skill training by keeping abreast with latest developments in the skills space.

C) Skilling will be integrated with formal education by introducing vocational training classes linked to the local economy from class 9 onwards in at least 25 percent of the schools, over the next five years. Seamless integration of vocational training in formal education is expected to ignite student interest. All the National Skills Qualifications Framework (NSQF)–compliant assessment and certification bodies will be competent to provide support to the school boards for assessment and certification of the skilling component of vocational education and training wherever required.

D) Skilling will be increasingly integrated with higher education with polytechnics offering NSQF-aligned vocational courses and bachelor of vocational studies degrees. These courses will be aligned to a credit framework that can provide horizontal and vertical mobility. Furthermore, at least 25 percent of all existing institutions of higher education would offer add-on career-oriented courses with specialized skills at an appropriate NSQF level within the next five years.

E) The Industrial Training Institute (ITI) qualifications will be linked to formal educational qualification at appropriate level through suitable language/bridge courses as necessary in consultation with state/central boards of education. The existing ITIs and polytechnics will be modernized with courses and curriculum that are aligned to the emerging competency-based demand in the market. Technology would be leveraged for designing curricula and developing pedagogical techniques. ITIs interface with industry will be promoted to enhance apprenticeship opportunities, improve relevance of training, and increase employability of trainees. Industry is expected to take a lead role in running ITIs through Institute Management Committees (IMCs), which will be given autonomy to implement decisions in the interest of better training outcomes. Performance rating of ITIs will also be promoted based on outcome-linked parameters and trainee/ employer feedback.

F) Government will promote use of certified, skilled manpower for its work and projects through enabling provisions in their contracts. Industry will also be encouraged to follow suit and pay skill premium to skilled and semiskilled workers. The companies will also be asked to indicate the percentage of certified, skilled workforce in their units as a part of their annual report.

G) To further the aspiration and respect associated with skilling, National Skill Awards will be instituted in close association with major stakeholders. Participation of India at international platforms will be encouraged to showcase the skilling talent in the country. Moreover, a "National Skills Day" will be declared to annually commemorate and celebrate skilling through skill fairs and camps across the country.

H) Counselling and guidance have emerged as the biggest challenges in the skill space today. Good counselling will be useful to create aspiration and reduce the attrition rates during training and employment by help-ing candidates make informed choices. The vast network of existing Post Offices and Citizen Service Centers (CSCs) would be leveraged with industry support to create such a support system for the youth. Furthermore, the network of 285,000 Youth Clubs/Mahila Mandals of Nehru Yuva Kendras with presence in 623 districts would also facil-itate in providing counselling and guidance to the youth of the coun-try about various skilling programs and opportunities. Similarly, the cross-country network of volunteers of Nehru Yuva Kendra Sangathan and National Service Scheme will also be utilized to create awareness and build a favorable pro-skilling environment among the youth in the country. These agencies will be provided with necessary brochures and other material for dissemination of required information through its volunteers among the target audience.

I) The Prime Minister's Skill Development Fellow scheme will be introduced to tap talented, young individuals who will work with the state and district administration to spread awareness about skill development, identify the local needs, and steer skill development efforts in the region.

Capacity

The annual skilling in the country was estimated at around 7 million in 2014. In the current landscape, capacity is being created by private sector training organizations, industry in-house training, government and private ITIs, Advanced Training Institutes (ATIs), tool rooms, and schools, colleges, and polytechnics. For all existing and new capacity that will be generated, the focus will move from inputs to outcomes of skill training that include employability and placements of trainees. Incentives will be linked to placement in all training institutions. For government-supported schemes, funding will be linked to outcomes of training programs.

A) Government will support the creation and use of infrastructure in both public and private domains through appropriate equity, grant, and loan support. It will continue to encourage entrepreneurs to enter into the skill training space by providing milestone-linked funding support through existing and new institutional mechanisms. For ensuring greater accessibility and equity, a targeted approach of preferential empanelment, approval, and funding of training providers will be put into place for the sectors and geographies where training capacity is clearly inadequate. Appropriate public-private partnership (PPP) models will be promoted to expand capacities in unserved areas.

B) India has a tremendous amount of hard and soft infrastructure that is underutilized. For instance, there are over 1,000,000 institutional buildings that are used for less than 40 hours a week. Skilling is a challenge that requires the supply to be close to the skill catchment; thus, it is essential to take skilling to the remotest parts of the country and scale up quickly, which is only possible by using this existing infrastructure. By designing suitable incentive schemes, existing infrastructure both in terms of buildings and potential teachers would be optimally leveraged for skill training. There are over 1.55 million schools, 25,000 colleges, 3,200 polytechnics, 83 youth hostels, around 150,000 post offices, and over 100,000 kiosks across the country. Schools/colleges will be used during holidays/off-hours for training purposes; shop floors of industries will be utilized for practical training and so on. Existing institutions in the agriculture sector such as Krishi Vigyan Kendras, agro-business clinics, and Indian Council of Agriculture Research (ICAR) will be utilized for providing skill training as well. There is availability of 65,000 kms of railway network in the country with over 8,000 stations, out of which a large proportion have adequate infrastructure facilities, electricity supply, and an extensive fiber optic cable (FOC) network. The possibility of leveraging this to deliver short-term skilling courses and promoting awareness would be explored. Branding of the Skill India Initiative will also be ensured through railways.

C) New ITIs will be set up in PPP mode, especially in unserved blocks of the country to expand the outreach of skilling programs. Furthermore, higher-order skilling will be promoted through ATIs and Multiskill Institutes (MSIs) set up in PPP mode with strong industry linkages. These institutes will focus on long-term skilling (one to three years) and will be located near the demand centers as skill hubs fostering apprenticeship and placements. These institutes will be affiliated to skill universities to provide general higher education through diplomas/certificates based on a credit framework to the appropriate NSQF level. They will function in a hub-and-spoke model to ensure greater outreach. A network of spokes in the form of livelihood colleges/ITIs/ITCs/private training centers already exist across the country and will be further promoted to focus on imparting employable skills up to NSQF Level 4. This model will drive accessibility and flexibility of skills training programs and ensure that it is able to draw on the research required to deliver world-class training.

D) Special focus will be laid on youth who do not wish to continue with school or higher education so that they are provided skills for other sustainable livelihood options. Special programs will be initiated for providing skill training to those who have 8 years or more of schooling. Separate skill courses, aligned to the appropriate NSQF levels, will be held in existing schools/centers during evening hours to provide alternate career pathway to these students. NSQF as a means to integrate and provide multiple pathways between general and vocational education will help school dropouts make choices about vocational courses.

E) State governments would be encouraged to setup Kaushal Vardhan Kendras (KVKs) at panchayat level for mobilizing and imparting skills pertaining to local employment/livelihood opportunities to school dropouts, adolescent girls, housewives, and rural youth. Each KVK will be linked to the nearest ITI/MSI/ATI for capacity-building, curriculum development, assessment, and certification. The KVKs will also function as counselling and guidance centers for youth to help them make informed choices. NGOs will also be empanelled for running these centers in their areas of operation. Some state governments are already working in this direction. Their efforts would be further encouraged to ensure setting up of at least one KVK in each block within the country over next five years.

F) The human resource requirements of the country will be addressed by aligning the supply and composition of skilled workers with demand. Training providers will be incentivized and government schemes will be designed and implemented to enable the workforce to benefit from the requirements of industry and the country's strategic priorities, including flagship programs. This will ensure that the supply of skilled workforce is relevant to projected needs and can be easily absorbed into the job market.

G) Private sector initiatives in skilling will be encouraged and would be entrusted to National Skill Development Corporation (NSDC) to create skilling capacity in the country. For this purpose, NSDC would continue to catalyze the creation of market-based, scalable business by providing patient funding through a combination of debt, equity, and grants to private sector to build capacity. This capacity would be created on self-sustainable model through private training partners to cater to skilling needs of educational dropouts in rural and urban landscape to bring them back to sustainable livelihood options.

H) The apprenticeship opportunities in the country are presently insignificant when compared to the size of the economy. Government has carried out comprehensive reforms in the Apprentices Act, 1961, to make it both industry- and youth-friendly. Government will work together with industry, including micro, small, and medium enterprises (MSME) sector, to create a positive environment for increased apprenticeship opportunities in the country. The services sector will also be brought under the ambit of apprenticeship. Apprenticeship will further be incentivized in the MSME sector through appropriate schemes for sharing of stipend and so on. Government will target a 10-fold increase in apprenticeship opportunities in the next five years.

Quality

"One Nation One Standard" should become the mantra to ensure that national standards and quality for skilling are globally aligned and Indian youth can aspire to secure local, national, and international job opportunities. Quality of training can be measured by competency outcomes and employability of trainees. The following parameters have been identified for improving quality:

A) Quality assurance (QA) framework embedded in NSQF
B) Market-relevant training programs
C) Recognition of prior learning (RPL)
D) Curriculum alignment
E) National Certification Framework
F) Employability skills
G) Placements.

Quality Assurance

A) A quality assurance (QA) framework embedded in NSQF will be finalized within next one year. This will build trust and confidence in the system by putting in place mechanisms that ensure the qualifications (and related training) produce consistent quality outcomes and are relevant to the labor market. It will ensure that training providers have the capacity to deliver training that meets quality requirements. The QA framework will improve the consistency of outcomes linked to certification and, consequently, improve the status of skills training. It would also lay down the framework for independent assessment and certification system in the country. It will also promote use of Skill India logo by certifying bodies (those conforming to QA framework) on their certificates, which can ensure national and international recognition of outcomes certified.
B) All formal and vocational education including skill training will have to align themselves with NSQF by December 2018. It is a nationally

integrated education- and competency-based skill framework that will provide for multiple pathways, horizontal as well as vertical, within vocational education, vocational training, general education, and technical education, thus linking one level of learning to another higher level. This would facilitate both horizontal and vertical mobility with formal education on outcome-based equivalence linked to a uniform credit framework. A legal framework to support NSQF will also be put in place.

C) The QA framework for certification and assessment will set minimum standards and provide guidance for effective, valid, reliable, fair, and transparent assessment within the context of the NSQF.

D) E-assessment would be encouraged wherever feasible to scale up capacity and increase convenience. Complete transparency and accountability will be ensured in the assessment process by leveraging technology. CCTV-monitored examinations and biometric attendance will be encouraged through appropriate incentives to compliant entities where government support or funding is involved. A central repository of all assessments conducted and certificates issued will be maintained on the national portal. The central repository, in addition to being available to employers, will also be available to candidates to enable them to track their performance and future up-skilling options.

E) Consolidated guidelines for accreditation of training providers, based on training capabilities, infrastructure, availability of trainers, tie-up with industry, and so on will be notified. This will facilitate accreditation at multiple levels and for multiple courses. The accreditation will be revised periodically to help students to make informed choices about the training providers.

F) Assessment ecosystem will also be strengthened through a framework for accreditation of assessing bodies and evaluation of assessors, to ensure consistent outcomes.

Market-led Standards

Sector Skills Councils (SSCs), as industry-led bodies, will be strengthened by making them more representative, expanding their outreach and increasing their efficiency. The development of National Occupational Standards (NOS) and Qualification Packs (QPs) for various job roles in a sector will remain the key responsibility of the SSCs. The outcome standards for each job role will need to be clearly defined and notified as per NSQF. SSCs will be responsible for ensuring that persons trained as per NOS/ QPs are employed by employers in their sector. 4.3.9 Development of standards by SSCs will be under the aegis of National Skills Qualification Committee (NSQC) under NSQF. All NOSs and QPs developed by the SSCs will be examined and reviewed by the NSQC and thereafter, con-ferred the status of "National Standards." All skill training in the country will necessarily align itself to these national standards.

Recognition of Prior Learning (RPL)

RPL is the key instrument that can help map the existing skills in the unorganized sector and integrate the informal sector to the formal skilling landscape. The RPL framework is an outcome-based qualification framework linked to NSQF against which prior learning through formal/ informal channels would be assessed and certified. The RPL process would include a preassessment, skill gap training and final assessment leading to certification of existing skills in an individual. The RPL certification would be at par with the certifications following various skill trainings in the country. It will provide both horizontal and vertical pathways to an individual for acquiring additional skills for better livelihoods. Adequate resources will be earmarked under various government schemes for equitable access to RPL programs. Government will provide detailed guidelines for RPL initiatives to ensure quality and consistent outcomes.

Creating a Dynamic and Demand-driven Curriculum Framework

The curriculum development will be promoted through sector mentor committees, which will include representatives from concerned SSCs, sector experts, and relevant academia, to ensure that the curriculum is in sync with emerging market demands and aligned to latest NOSs and QPs. The curriculum should also take into account the latest teaching aids that can be used to disseminate quality training on a large scale. The curriculum will need to be reviewed every 3 years to align itself with the dynamic market needs. In addition, industry will be allowed to run high-employment-potential courses through appropriate affiliation framework.

National Certification Framework

Presently, the National Council for Vocational Training (NCVT), constituted in 1956, provides a national framework for setting curricula for various vocational courses and also prescribes standards for equipment, scale of space, duration of courses, methods of training, conducting All India Trade Tests, and awarding National Trade Certificates. NCVT will be further strengthened by scaling up industry representation through SSCs and laying down a national framework for all certification in the skill space through an autonomous body.

Employability Skills

Language and basic IT and financial literacy is an integral part of most job roles in the economy today. Furthermore, life skills are also an integral to a successful livelihood. Accordingly, all skill training programs shall include basic modules of computer literacy, finance, language, and soft skills like etiquettes, appreciating gender diversity in workplace, building positive health attitudes, and social and life skills to enable the youth to be employable and market-ready.

Placements

The most critical outcome of skill training is employment, whether self- or wage employment. To assess quality of skill training, this critical outcome will need to be monitored objectively. Employment tracking of individuals for at least 1 year, postskill training, will be made mandatory under all skill programs.

Synergy

Skill development programs being implemented by various ministries/departments/agencies of the central government have different norms as regards the eligibility criteria, duration of training, maximum funds needed for training, outcomes, monitoring and tracking mechanism, and so on. This multiplicity of norms and parameters results in avoidable difficulties in implementation and makes it difficult to evaluate the performance of the skill development programs across the central government in an objective manner.

A) Ministry of Skill Development and Entrepreneurship (MSDE), which has been set up to coordinate skill development efforts in the country will, within 3 months, notify common norms for rationalization of central government schemes on skill development. The norms shall include standards for inputs/output, funding/cost norms, third-party certification, assessment cost, and so on across the various skill development programs while allowing flexibility to meet the requirements of different parts of the country/different socioeconomic groups. However, different ministries will be free to frame schemes at their discretion to meet local/sectoral needs while adhering to common norms.

B) A national Labour Market Information System (LMIS) will be created. This will be an integrated database, which contains socioeconomic data in modules on (i) supply-side skilled labor force statistics, (ii) demand of skilled/unskilled labor, (iii) market trends like wage structures and distribution, economic growth trends across sectors, focus areas for skilled manpower, and occupational shortages. The LMIS is expected to use a business intelligence tool to generate key analysis and reports that will determine policy interventions by different government stakeholders and the industry at large. It will help inform candidates about the choices available to them in terms of sectors, modules, and training providers leading them to better career opportunities. In addition, LMIS will cater to the following stakeholders: trainees, training providers, industry/employers, government agency/policymakers, assessment agencies, certifying agencies, funding agencies, international agencies, Sector Skill Councils, labor-market-tracking agencies, and placement agencies. It is being developed in a modular manner. It will integrate all existing databases like NSDC's Skill Development Management System (SDMS), National Career Service Portal,

National Council for Vocational Training (NCVT) MIS portal, Skill Development Initiative Scheme (SDIS) portal, state databases, and SSC databases.

C) LMIS will be part of the larger national portal, which will also include details on skills courses, e-content, sector reports, trainers, assessors, and so on. Data for all the persons mobilized and seeking skill training will be entered into the national portal. It will be ensured that the national portal is user-friendly and is available in relevant regional languages to ensure that language does not become a barrier to access information. The system would be used for forecasting future demand and accordingly preparing a constant flow of skilled workforce. Furthermore, all data will be maintained in gender-disaggregated form to enable specific policy interventions to maintain equity.

D) States will also be encouraged to converge all skill development activities under a single entity on the pattern of State Skill Development Missions (SSDMs) as already being implemented in a few states. They will also be requested to synergize their skill programs with common norms as notified by the central government in order to maintain uniformity in the entire skilling space. Skill database of states will also be integrated with LMIS to have a unified national picture of actual supply against demand in various sectors.

Skill India and Make in India

Make in India and Skill India are complementary to each other. The key objective of Make in India is to promote manufacturing in 25 sectors of the economy, which will lead to job creation and, consequently, the need for skilled manpower. Some of these sectors include automobiles, chemicals, IT, pharmaceuticals, textiles, ports, aviation, leather, tourism and hospitality, wellness, railways, auto components, design manufacturing, renewable energy, mining, biotechnology, and electronics. Correspondingly, Skill India aims at preparing a highly skilled workforce that is completely aligned to the requirements of industry so as to promote growth through improved productivity.

A) Skilling efforts will be completely aligned with the requirements of 25 key identified sectors of Make in India. A joint committee of stakeholders under both initiatives will be constituted to closely monitor growth of manufacturing activity under the Make in India program and anticipate skill requirements for such initiatives so that the same can be developed in coordination with various SSCs and training institutions. Preassessment of skill requirements for all manufacturing activities at proposal stage will be made mandatory in order to ensure an industry-ready workforce once the manufacturing facilities have been set up. States will also be encouraged to align their skilling efforts with upcoming industrial activities in the state.

B) Make in India could be leveraged to increase industry participation in skills through PPP mode, namely, setting up ATIs/MSIs with priority Make in India projects.

C) All new industrial/development clusters will be mandated to set up quality training institutes in the area to take care of skilling needs of the region.

Mobilization and Engagement

Industry needs to be closely involved in providing job opportunities to the skilled workforce. Industry will be encouraged to increasingly move toward employing only certified skilled people. In addition, employers need to rationalize the compensation paid across different levels of skills to award a skill premium for increased productivity as a result of higher skills.

A) Skill development is a shared responsibility of both the government and the industry. Since industry is one of the major stakeholders, it needs to actively contribute to the cause of skill development. The industry should earmark at least 2 percent of its payroll bill (including for contract labor) for skill development initiatives in their respective sector. These funds can be channelized for skill development activities either through the respective SSCs or through National Skill Development Fund (NSDF).

B) Industry should actively participate in designing curricula and standards for skill training courses. Industry members will be requested to contribute as guest faculty at ITIs, ATIs, MSIs, and other skill training institutes. Industry houses, including the MSMEs, will be incentivized to make shop floor available for practical training of trainees and institutionalize paid apprenticeship. Workplace training will be promoted as part of the overall skill curriculum aligned to NSQF and embedded in appropriate credit framework. Industry will also be encouraged to participate more actively in training of youth, so that the latter are able to get actual on-the-job and hands-on experience during training programs.

C) Every training provider, including ITIs, should tie up with industry in the relevant trades to improve placement opportunities for candidates. Similarly, every industry should also tie up with suitable training center(s) in its vicinity for supply of skilled workforce and apprentices. There should be a placement-cum-apprenticeship cell within each training center that will counsel trainees on successful completion of their training and help them get employed. Industry mentors will be assigned wherever possible to trainees of government-supported schemes. The aforesaid cell will maintain a complete database of all trainees and their employment record thereafter. Government support to training providers would be linked to placement performance and tie-ups with industry.

D) Special efforts will be made to organize and streamline efforts of the nongovernmental (NGO) sector in their skill development initiatives. Mentorship support will be provided to eligible NGOs through NSDC to scale and create sustainable models for skill development for green jobs (agriculture, horticulture, renewable energy, recycling, ecotourism, etc.), grey-collar jobs (informal manufacturing and services), and local trades, especially in rural India, through Krishi Vijnana Kendras (KVK).

Global Partnerships

The main objective of global partnerships and international collaborations is to leverage best practices from across the world. Such collaborations will immensely enrich domestic training programs by enhancing their quality through learnings from successful international models of vocational-ization of education, engaging with industry, and so on. Institutional arrangements through joint working groups, secretariats, and so on will be established for regular exchange of knowledge, experiences, research findings, teaching and learning materials, and innovations in skill development.

A) Foreign governments, corporate entities, and training organizations will also be encouraged to set up skill centers and universities as well as participate in content creation, design of curriculum, and delivery of training. Exchange and capacity-building programs for teachers, administrators, and students will be facilitated.

B) Government would promote a skills training ecosystem that would also enable training and placement of Indian youth in overseas jobs. The ageing developed world is expected to face a huge skill shortage while our country has the potential to reap its demographic advan-tage and export skilled labor to the world. A focused team would be formulated for identification of countries and trades where skill short-ages exist or are likely to develop in near future.

C) According to U.S. Census Bureau estimate, by 2022, countries like the United States, the United Kingdom, and China will fall short of the required skilled labor by 17 million, 2 million, and 10 million, respectively, while India will have a surplus of almost 47 million work-force in the age group of 19 to 59 years. This strength can be leveraged by countries of destination to meet their labor and skill shortages. Labor mobility is the only long-term solution for sustaining global growth rates. To address this aspect of skill mobility the government will proactively build human resource mobility partnerships (HRMP) with key countries in collaboration with the concerned parties.

D) Currently, there are about 14 million Indians employed overseas, 70 percent of whom are unskilled or semiskilled laborers. Due to several reasons, such as lack of skills, inadequate information, lack of knowledge of basic language, they often have to work in adverse circumstances with biased terms of employment. To address the existing issues faced by Indian laborers abroad, government will further enhance the scheme of skill upgradation and predeparture orientation training to emigrant workers. The scheme will have the objective of institutionalizing the process of skill development of emigrant workers and to equip them with the basic knowledge about laws, language, and culture of the destination countries for the purpose of overseas employment.

E) The NSQF will be aligned to globally recognized qualification frameworks for ensuring quality and uniformity. Consequently, transnational standards will be created for sectors where employment opportunity exists for international workforce mobility. Close partnerships with the concerned countries would enable certified Indian youth to get employed in these countries. Assessment and certification framework will be benchmarked to international standards. National Skills Qualification Committee (NSQC), with assistance from the concerned SSCs, would be capacitated to develop working standards, assessments, and certifications with respective agencies in the destination countries.

F) In addition, there are countries and regions where India will support development of skill development ecosystem through sharing its institutional models, occupational standards, and qualification packs.

Outreach

The proposed KVKs will play a pivotal role in identifying local employment opportunities and providing adequate training and posttraining support according to needs of local areas, such as migration support for skilled workers. The centers will also function as information centers for training and employment opportunities as well as for various support schemes. KVKs in the form of mobile training facilities will also be deployed to reach out to remote and difficult areas.

A) More than 93 percent of India's workforce is in the unorganized sector. Hence, strengthening and certifying the skills of the unorganized workforce will contribute to overall economic development of this sector. RPL will be encouraged in the unorganized sector for certification of existing skills and integration with formal labor market. This will also open up options for up-skilling and further vertical mobility. Multiskilling in complementary areas will be promoted to enable sustainable livelihood in this sector.

B) To develop the unorganized sector, LMIS will be used to aggregate the availability of labor with certified skill levels to help some of them move to organized sector. Technology will be also be leveraged for the aggregation of informal sector workers through mobile-based IT applications and link them directly to the job market and also make them accessible to prospective employers. Efforts will be made to include details of skill training and skilled manpower working in the unorganized and MSME sectors through periodic sample surveys of the National Sample Survey Office (NSSO).

C) An unrecognized apprentice system or on-the-job training exists in the informal sector. The RPL program will enable trainees/apprentices at such informal establishments to obtain certification and access to add-on classes. If required, financial support could be provided for such efforts.

D) Government believes that inability to pay training fees should not stop any citizen from acquiring certified skill training. Government will promote grant of scholarships, rewards, and skill vouchers (SV) for funding of training costs. All desirous candidates would be able to access credit for all certified NSQF-aligned skill development programs through targeted SVs that will be linked to their Aadhaar and their Jan Dhan Account or bank account. Levy from future incomes would be linked for recovery of loans through SVs. This is proposed to promote an environment of "Learn, Earn, and Pay." SVs can be redeemed by training providers based on performance-linked payment schedule subject to successful completion of training. Scholarships and grants up to 100 percent linked to SVs will also be provided for certain identified disadvantaged sections of society. However, 30 percent of any grant will be linked to continuous employment for at least 1 year.

E) A National Skills Research Division (NSRD) will be constituted within NSDA at the national level. The role of the division will be to conduct skill surveys including aggregation of the environmental scans done by SSCs, study emerging demand trends, and operate the LMIS and other skilling platforms and databases. This body will have close involvement of private sector subject experts and will be the strategy think-tank for MSDE. It will also keep a close watch on developments taking place internationally in these areas and align our policy response to enable engagement with various stakeholders in the skilling ecosystem and ensure that skill sets of our people are also aligned with international requirements/benchmark, ensuring their global mobility.

F) A national campaign, including through a dedicated TV and radio channel, and skilling camps will be initiated to promote interest and mobilize the youth for skilling. Timely circulation of success stories in electronic as well as print media will also be ensured.

ICT Enablement

Promotion of only brick-and-mortar facilities will not ensure the speed and scale desired to transform the skill development efforts. The use of technology will be leveraged to scale up training facilities, enable access to remote areas, and increase cost-effectiveness of delivery of vocational training. Government will also look to support innovative products, solutions, and models that address critical gaps in skill ecosystem in an effective manner. Use of existing available networks such as the widespread optical fiber network will be optimized.

A) An open platform for e-content on skill development will be created where further curated content will be crowd-sourced. Mechanisms will be put in place to incentivize high-quality content aggregation. This platform would provide standardized training content to be used by trainers/training institutes for delivery of vocational training. Stakeholders will be encouraged to develop massive open online courses (MOOC) and virtual classrooms for easy access and convenience. Creation of blended learning environments to deliver high-quality vocational training in underserved regions of India will be promoted. Curriculum and teaching methodologies for online learning tools will be provided in regional languages to cater to the various geographical needs.

B) As discussed elsewhere, a responsive and agile central LMIS will be created for aggregating demand and supply of skills to help align efforts toward bridging the existing and expected skill gaps. The LMIS will be responsible for a reliable and realistic assessment of economic trends and labor market needs (both existing and projected) that will be publicly available to reduce information asymmetry.

C) There are approximately 900 million cell phone users in the country, of which 120 million use smartphones. Location services capability has added another layer in communication and value. It is thus possible to have high-end data collection and assimilation for intelligent matching. The government aims to promote in private domain a matching online/mobile platform for connecting supply and demand of skilled workers. Private sector will be encouraged to develop mobile applications for aggregating informal sector workers for household services, such as plumbers, carpenters, and so on, through innovative commercial models.

D) Government envisions to leverage the facility of digital locker for creation of skill cards linked to Aadhaar for the labor force trained and certified as per NSQF. The skill cards will be a portable, online record of an individual's education, qualifications, competencies, Aadhaar, employment history, training record, and objectives, details of which can be independently verified. Skill cards shall reduce duplication of training, simplify statutory and mandatory training, and provide an overview of the skills and abilities of the entire workforce. The work performance of the worker can also be rated by trainers or employers, which can act as a signaling mechanism.

E) Technology would be leveraged in monitoring of government schemes related to skill development—including the entire ecosystem—from the government agency to the training provider to the trainee to the financial transactions.

F) To meet the objective of making skilling aspirational, networks and special interest groups will be created through advanced and easily accessible technological tools, in order to spread awareness and increase outreach.

Trainers and Assessors

To achieve the massive target of skilling, it is of utmost importance to have quality trainers who are capable of training people in several fields. Similarly, quality assessors in sufficient numbers are also required to ensure consistent outcomes of assessment and certification process. Government will decisively intervene directly or through other stakeholders, to bring more experienced people in training and assessment space, especially ex-servicemen in defense and retired/working people from industry.

A) A trainer/assessor portal will be set up as a part of the national portal to act as a repository and registration database for all certified and interested trainers/assessors. All retiring employees in industry or government domain, who are interested to use their experience gainfully by extending their career as trainers/assessors, will have freedom to register themselves on the portal. This portal can be easily accessed by training providers and assessment bodies as per their relevant sector, experience, and location of the registered certified trainers/ assessors.

B) Short-term modules for training of interested persons, with relevant industry experience, will be promoted through instructor training institutes to enable them to attain the requisite certification for being a certified trainer/assessor. Career pathways will be redefined for trainers to make the profession more attractive and lucrative for the youth. The job of skill trainers will be made aspirational by benchmarking their pay scales with secondary-school teachers.

C) New institutes for training of trainers will be set up in PPP mode, at least one in each state, to increase the overall capacity of ToT in the country. With increase in availability of certified trainers, all training institutes will be mandated to engage certified trainers only.

D) As a part of the promotion of industry–institute linkage, working industry professionals would also be empanelled as adjunct faculty in relevant areas during off-hours.

E) Centers of excellence, under the proposed national skills universities, will also be set up to ensure continuous supply of quality trainers in each sector. Special training programs would be developed for training of trainers meant for overseas employment, including language training in collaboration with the concerned country. This could include exchange programs, industry visits, and simulated training. ICT-enabled training and certification program for the trainers to train them within comforts of their homes, wherever feasible would also be promoted. Moreover, appropriate training in the latest technological developments for upgrading the technical skill of trainers, as per the requirement of the present scenario, will also be provided by the industry.

F) In the defense sector, it is estimated that 50,000 armed forces personnel retire every year with majority of them in the age group of 35 to 45 years. MSDE through its institutions will work with the Directorate General of Resettlement (DGR) to provide them future livelihood opportunities through skill training in sectors where their experience can be put to good use, including as trainers and assessors.

Inclusivity

It is necessary to promote skill development initiatives that will ensure inclusivity, irrespective of gender, location, caste, sector, and so on. One of the key objectives is to safeguard the skilling needs of SCs, STs, OBCs, minorities, and differently abled persons, as well as those living in difficult geographical pockets.

A) Government attaches high priority to socioeconomic growth of rural areas since India lives in her villages. Adequate focus will be given to youth from deprived households by establishing skill development centers in underserved areas.

B) The border, hilly and difficult areas, including North-Eastern states, Jammu and Kashmir, and the hilly forested areas of Central and Eastern India face additional challenges arising from inadequate infrastructure, poor investment, and low industrial opportunities. Special attention needs to be given to youth residing in these regions to address their needs for employment and employability. In order to provide more equitable access across the country, special efforts, including earmarking of funds for establishing training facilities in deficient regions and need-based subsidization of skill training for disadvantaged groups, will be initiated. Natural aptitude of youth will also be kept in view while implementing training programs in these geographies.

C) Areas such as North-Eastern States, Jammu and Kashmir, and Himachal Pradesh face peculiar problems that are different from the rest of the country. Comparatively, there are very few training centers in the entire North-East region. Youth in such regions seek jobs but are not complemented with adequate job opportunities in the region. Government will create special regional structures for difficult areas, which will be cross-sectoral, and work closely with SSCs to address the existing problems of such sensitive regions with aptitude-based training and employment.

D) For differently abled persons, a horizontal SSC comprising of stakeholders and representatives of relevant SSCs would be created to identify specific trades for each category of differently abled candidates where they can improve their competencies through skill training and get rehabilitated/employed for a sustainable livelihood.

E) Government will allow flexibility in various skill schemes to address special needs of various sections of society through innovative models within the overall architecture of the scheme. Skill training will be aligned to specific requirements of the community and local ecosystem. Earmarking of funds for disadvantaged sections of society like SC, ST, and minorities will be enforced as per existing government guidelines. Existing schemes for disadvantaged groups will be further strengthened and made more effective.

Promotion of Skilling among Women

According to Census Data 2001, women account for 48 percent of the entire population in India. Women have the capability to further drive the economy of the country if their participation in the workforce is increased. With the help of skilling, women can have viable incomes, decent work, and be major players who can contribute equally to the economic growth of the country.

A) Women participation in vocational education and training is especially low compared to men. Special mechanisms in the delivery of training such as mobile training units, flexible afternoon batches, training based on the local needs of the area will be introduced to ensure participation and mobilization of women. Government will promote setting up of more training and apprenticeship seats exclusively for women. Appropriate incentive mechanism will be designed to achieve the same.

B) Training in nontraditional fields for women will be promoted through the establishment of specific training program that focus on life skills training modules and literacy training. Apart from that, efforts will be made to increase the pool of women trainers and providing them certification by earmarking a certain percentage of intake in training-of-trainers institutes for women. New institutes exclusively for training of women as trainees and trainers will also be promoted by the government.

C) Women-related issues will be incorporated in the guidelines for skill training procedures. These could include issues of safe and gender-sensitive training environment, employment of women trainers, equity in remuneration, and complaint redressal mechanism.

D) An Internet- or mobile-based platform for women employment, by connecting skilled women and employers, will be promoted. This platform could focus on women willing to reenter the workforce after a break and those affected by migration.

Governance Structures and Processes

While the policy framework for skill development and entrepreneurship has been clearly enshrined, the policy further spells out a governance structure for effective and efficient implementation of program goals and objectives (National Policy of Skill Development and Entrepreneurship 2015). National Skill Development Mission, under the MSDE, is visualized to implement and coordinate all skilling efforts in the country toward the objectives laid down in the policy. The mission will consist of a governing council at apex level and a steering committee and a mission directorate (along with an executive committee) as the executive arm of the mission.

Mission directorate will be supported by three other institutions—National Skill Development Agency (NSDA), National Skill Development Corporation (NSDC), and Directorate General of Training (DGT)—all of which will have horizontal/vertical linkages with the mission directorate to facilitate smooth functioning of the national institutional mechanism.

In order to ensure that skill development efforts being made by all stakeholders in the system are in accordance with actual needs of industry, Sector Skill Councils (SSCs) are being set up. SSCs are industry-led and industry-governed bodies, which will help link the requirements of industry with appropriately trained manpower.

Besides, functional collaborations with entrepreneurship institutions, including National Institute for Entrepreneurship and Small Business Development (NIESBUD) and Indian Institute of Entrepreneurship (IIE), are proposed in order to promote training, consultancy, research and publication, and, in turn, entrepreneurship.

National Skill Development Corporation India (NSDC)

The National Skill Development Corporation India (NSDC) is a PPP organization (now under the MSDE) that was incorporated in 2009 under the National Skill Policy. Its main aim is to provide viability gap funding to private sector in order to scale up training capacity. NSDC has tied up with more than 187 training providers, many of whom have started scaling up their operations.

NSDC has also been entrusted to set up SSCs ensuring right representation of employers and to extend financial support to operationalize them. It also undertakes research initiatives, pilot projects, and skill gap studies to create a knowledge base for the sector. They have supported and incubated 31 SSCs that are intended to facilitate the much-needed participation and ownership of the industry to ensure needs-based training programs. NSDC's mandate also involves capacity building by working with different stakeholders and identifying best practices to create an excellence model. The NSDC has also been working to create awareness about the skill ecosystem and has rolled out electronic and print campaigns.

National Skills Development Agency (NSDA)

NSDA is working with the state governments to rejuvenate and synergize skilling efforts in the state. The National Skills Qualification Framework

(NSQF) has been anchored at NSDA, and efforts have been initiated to align all skilling and education outcomes with the competency-based NSQF levels.

Sector Skill Councils (SSC)

The National Skill Development Policy of 2009 mandated the NSDC to setup SSCs to bring together key stakeholders—industry, workforce, and academia. As of now, 29 SSCs are operational and 4 more SSCs have been approved by NSDC. They are funded by NSDC for the initial few years and are expected to become financially self-sustaining as they grow.

These SSCs are expected to lay down the National Occupational Standards (NOS) for different levels of jobs in their respective sectors, formulate certification and accreditation norms, strive to create knowledge repository on current requirement of skill development in the industry, assess the supply of skilled workers, identify the demand and supply gap in each sector, and identify trends and future requirements. With availability of trainers being a major challenge in scaling up the capacity, SSCs are also expected to play a crucial role in getting the right industry support to facilitate training of trainers for their respective sectors.

National Council for Vocational Training (NCVT)

Established under Ministry of Labor and Employment with a view to ensure and maintain uniformity in the standards of training all over the country, the National Council for Vocational Training (NCVT) was set up in 1956. This certifying body conducts All India Trade Tests for those who complete training in ITIs and awards National Trade Certificates to successful candidates. The council has representation from central and state government departments, employers' and workers' organizations, professional and learned bodies, All India Council for Technical Education, SCs and STs, All India Women's Organization, among others. The State Council for Vocational Training (SCVT) at the state levels and the subcommittees have been established to assist the national council.

Quality Council of India (QCI)

The Quality Council of India (QCI) was set up jointly by the Government of India and the Indian industry as an autonomous body to establish a national accreditation structure in the field of education, health care, environment protection, governance, social sectors, infrastructure, vocational training, and other areas that have significant bearing in improving the quality of life. All institutions (government and private ITIs) seeking formal affiliation from NCVT have to first get accreditation from the QCI.

National Skills Qualifications Framework (NSQF)

The NSQF is a competency-based framework that organizes all qualifications according to a series of levels of knowledge, skills, and aptitude. These levels, graded from 1 to 10, are defined in terms of learning outcomes that the learner must possess regardless of whether they are obtained through formal, nonformal, or informal learning. NSQF in India was notified on December 27, 2013. Government funding is also expected to be on preferential basis for NSQF-compliant training/educational programs/courses. The NSQF would facilitate a paradigm shift from education focused on inputs to an outcomes/competency-based education, which would help in the recognition of prior learning and simultaneously enable the alignment of the Indian qualifications with international ones. It is a competency-based framework that organizes qualifications into 10 levels, with the entry level being 1, and the highest level being 10. Each of these levels is characterized by the following categories of competencies:

1. Professional knowledge—what the person must know at that level
2. Professional skills—what the person should be able to do at that level
3. Core skills—which include soft and interpersonal skills
4. Responsibility—the degree of supervision that needs to be exercised over the person while doing the job or the degree of supervision that person is capable of exercising over others.

Awarding bodies submit their qualifications/courses to NSDA in order to seek approval from NSQC for NSQF alignment. The awarding bodies submit their information in a template called Qualification File. The Qualification File is the means by which awarding bodies present evidence to the National Skills Qualification Committee that their qualifications are NSQF-compliant.

NSDA plays a crucial role in operationalizing NSQF in the states. In the process of operationalizing of NSQF, e-kit of NSQF is delivered to the state nodal agency or SSDMs. Workshop on NSQF is done with the stakeholders of the state. Following this, a core committee on NSQF is constituted by the state that works out the alignment of state-specific qualifications to NSQF. Core committee on NSQF has been formed in 11 states: Assam, Haryana, Meghalaya, Punjab, Puducherry, Odisha, Nagaland, Tamil Nadu, Tripura, Uttarakhand, and Uttar Pradesh. Core committee is a committee comprising representatives from various state departments of the state that are expected to work on operationalizing NSQF in the state. This committee identifies state-specific qualifications and submits all the relevant information in a Qualification File template and submit it to NSQC for approval. NSQF workshops have been conducted across 26 states and Union Territories, which are Assam, Andhra Pradesh, Chandigarh, Dadra and Nagar Haveli, Daman, Delhi, Gujarat, Haryana, Himachal Pradesh, Jammu and Kashmir, Karnataka, Kerala, Maharashtra, Manipur, Meghalaya, Mizoram, Nagaland, Odisha, Puducherry, Rajasthan, Punjab, Sikkim, Tamil Nadu, Telengana, Tripura, Uttar Pradesh, Uttarakhand, and West Bengal. The states of Odisha, Telengana, Mizoram, and Haryana have also submitted few qualification files to NSDA for NSQF alignment.

National Labour Market Information System (N-LMIS)

NSDA has developed a single-window platform to aggregate supply-and-demand trends in the Indian vocational education and training space, referred to as the National Labour Market Information System (LMIS). The portal was formally launched by Honorable President of India on July 15, 2016. It is now known as Skill Exchange Labour Market Information System. LMIS is an integrated set of institutional arrangements, procedures, mechanisms, and data systems designed to produce labor market information as per global standards and best practices. The system brings together statistical (quantitative) and nonstatistical (qualitative) information concerning labor market actors and their environment and generate key analysis and reports that can be used for various policy interventions by different government stakeholders as well as by the industry at large. The data on the National LMIS is displayed in the form of 9 national repositories: trainers, training centers, training providers, assessors, assessment agencies, employers, trained candidates, courses, and prospective candidates each contributing to build a holistic picture of the skill development ecosystem in the country. As on date, 6.5 million trained candidate data from 4 different central ministries are reflected on the LMIS, which includes 7 major central skill development schemes. NSDA has developed a roadmap for integrating all remaining data sources, including states, central ministries, and other agencies working in the skill development space. The first step in this direction is to undertake a scoping study of all skill development MIS systems in the country that will be completed by June 2017. Following this study, NSDA will develop an action plan for state integration and roll-out, which will include strengthening of state and institutional MIS systems in a systematic, phased approach. The employment linkage on the LMIS has been facilitated through integration with the National Career Services Portal maintained by the Ministry of Labour and Employment. Through this integration, candidates trained and certified through government schemes and programs will be reflected as potential jobseekers on the NCS portal. NSDA has also initiated the process of signing a Memorandum of Understanding (MoU) with all major employment agencies and job portals for sharing of candidate data available on the national LMIS. As on date, NSDA has signed MoUs with Town Labour Technologies Ltd., Baba Jobs, Monster.com, and Saral Rozgar. This will ensure that candidates have multiple avenues facilitating employment linkages through the system.

The LMIS will make citizen services accessible over the Internet, through mobile phones, kiosks, and call centers as well as through personal computers, setting forward a vision for electronic service delivery that does not do away with the need for personal contact but rather supports better management with the infusion of technology. The system provides a consolidated and unified view of various stakeholders at any given point of time and empowers the government and agencies to take informed decisions by providing intelligent and insightful reports as required (Government of India, MSDE, *Annual Report*, 2016–2017).

Monitoring and Evaluation

The National Policy for Skill Development and Entrepreneurship has been structured as an outcome-oriented policy. It is therefore desirable that there be regular monitoring and evaluation of the initiatives to ensure that best practices can be scaled and corrective measures can be introduced. The main idea of having a robust monitoring and evaluation mechanism is to ensure successful implementation of policy initiatives.

Government desires to set up a Policy Implementation Unit (PIU) so as to review the implementation and progress of the various initiatives under this policy. The PIU will be housed in MSDE with secretary as the chairperson and representation from NITI Aayog. For the smooth functioning of the PIU, it will also ensure constant consultation with stakeholders to get feedback so as to enable improvements, if required. The PIU will perform the following functions:

- List all the action points as mentioned in the policy on which further action is required
- Identify all the agencies involved and map the actionable points to the responsible agency
- To coordinate with all the agencies involved and help them devise a draft outline as well as timelines for the implementation of the initiatives assigned to them
- Timelines that are explicitly mentioned in the policy for certain initiatives will supersede over other timelines
- To act as a coordinating body for all the implementing agencies and support them to enhance their efficiency
- The PIU will also conduct monthly review of the action points and nudge them if the progress is not as expected. The PIU will be made responsible to the NSDM. It will present its reports,

findings, and the way-forward to the steering committee of the mission every quarter. The PIU will be the main body overlooking the implementation of policy.

Impact Assessment

For the purpose of undertaking impact assessment, annual as well as five-year targets will be set for each stakeholder by the PIU. Impact assessment will be undertaken to ensure that the targets are met well within the timeframe. The stakeholders will also be subject to a quarterly review. For the purpose of impact assessment, the following monitoring indicators, among others, are prescribed:

A) Number/registrations of youth interested in skilling
B) Number of youth registered in training programs
C) Number of youth assessed and certified by regulatory authorities
D) Placement rate of skilled trainees
E) Number of accredited/affiliated training providers/centers
F) Number of certified trainers, sector-wise
G) Number of certified assessors, sector-wise
H) Number of job roles for which QPs and NOS have been developed
I) Existing public infrastructure leveraged for training
J) Number of skilled persons engaged in overseas employment
K) Reduction in sectoral demand–supply gap
L) Amount of private funds mobilized for encouraging skill development and entrepreneurship
M) Percentage of socially and geographically disadvantaged groups enrolled in training programs
N) Percentage of skilled youth that are self-employed
O) Infrastructure dedicated for entrepreneurship support
P) Number of schools running skills and entrepreneurship courses
Q) Percentage of socially and geographically disadvantaged groups engaged in self-employment

With the help of the PIU, it will be easier to monitor the implementation of the policy initiatives and take corrective measures in case of noncompliance. A mid-term review of the policy will be undertaken based on impact assessment by a third party. The policy can be considered for review after five years, based on learnings from the implementation of the policy.

Vocational Training Institutions in India

In India some of the training institutions in the formal system have played a major role in creating pool of skilled workers, which include ITIs, Industrial Training Centers (ITCs), polytechnics, community polytechnics, and community colleges (Tara and Kumar n.d.). The educational system of the country is presented in the following figure.

Industrial Training Institute (ITI)

The Craftsmen Training Scheme (CTS) was introduced in 1950 by the Directorate General of Employment and Training (DGE&T), Ministry

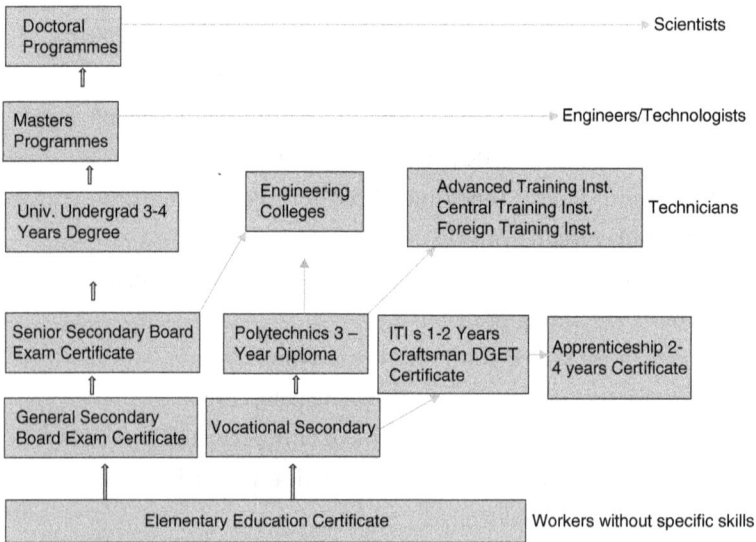

Education and training system in india

Source: Skill Development in India—The Vocational Education and Training System, Report No. 22, South Asia Human Development Sector, World Bank, January 2008.

of Labour, to ensure a steady flow of skilled workers in different trades for the domestic industry, to raise quantitatively and qualitatively industrial production by systematic training, to reduce unemployment among the educated youth by providing them employable skills, and to cultivate and nurture a technical and industrial attitude in the minds of younger generation. The scheme, the most important in the field of vocational training, has been shaping craftsmen to meet the existing as well as future manpower needs, through the vast network of ITIs in the various states/ union territories in the country. The government-owned ITIs and the private ITCs are the backbone of vocational education in India. In terms of student numbers, the ITIs are much larger, whereas most private ITCs offer only a few trades. Therefore, in some states, there are only dozens of it compared to hundreds of ITCs.

The growth in the number of ITIs over the years is appreciable. It started in a humble way in 1950 when 50 ITIs were opened. The second major phase of increase in ITIs came with the oil boom in West Asia and export of skilled manpower to that region from India. Several new private ITIs were established in the 1980s in Southern states such as Kerala, Karnataka, and Andhra Pradesh, from where trained craftsmen found placement mainly in the Gulf countries. In 1980, there were 831 ITIs and the number rose to 1,887 in 1987. During the 1990s, the growth of ITIs had been steep, and today there are over 8,687 ITIs/ITCs having a seating capacity of 1.21 million (*Annual Report*, 2010–2011, Ministry of Labour and Employment). The ITIs and ITCs deliver programs for the principal national training schemes, namely, the Craftsmen Training Scheme (CTS) and the Apprenticeship Training Scheme (ATS). As such, they cover 116 nationally recognized trades. The CTS provides medium- to long-term institutional training to produce semiskilled/skilled workers for industrial employment, whereas the ATS is a combined training program that offers both institutional and on-the-job training with the graduated apprentices being considered as skilled. The following table shows the number of government and private ITIs/ITCs in India with the seating capacity:

However, the quality of technical and vocational education imparted in these institutions in the country has been a matter of concern among policymakers. The challenge is to facilitate ITIs to keep pace with the fast-growing technological demands for industry and the expanding

Number of government and private ITIs/ITCs in India with the seating capacity

March 2016

All India	Number of government IT Is	Seating capacity (Government)	Number of private ITCs	Seating capacity (Private)	Total ITIs/ITCs	Total seating capacity
Total	2,293	505,618	10,812	1,360,002	13,105	1,865,620

Source: Data provided by MSDE, to a Parliamentary starred question (http://jaypanda.in/wp-content/uploads/2017/05/ITIs.pdf).

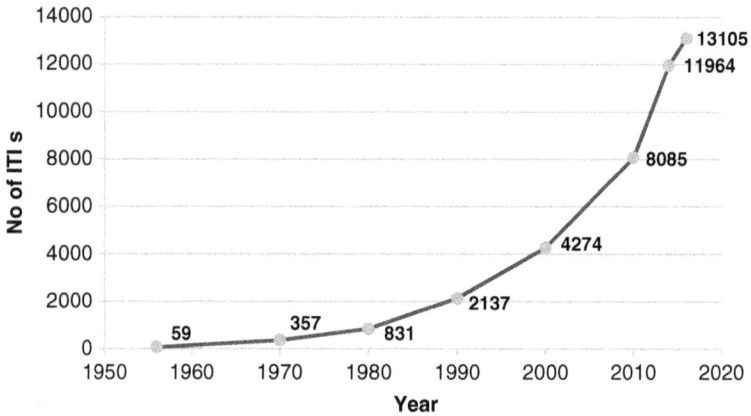

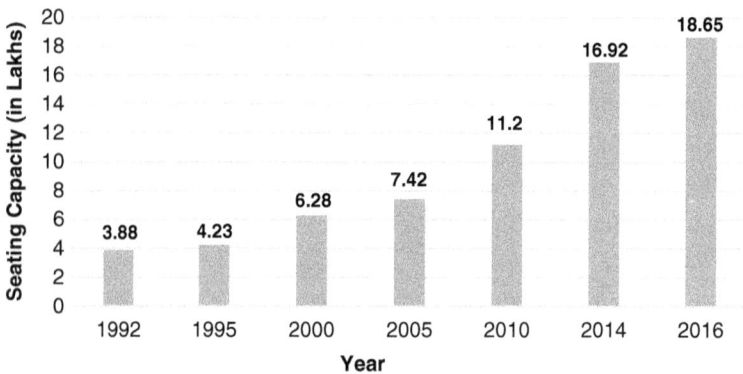

Source: http://dget.nic.in/content/institute/key-statistics.php

universe of knowledge. Furthermore, such an attempt to enhance the quality of training and training infrastructure through improved design and delivery system, especially in curriculum development, capacity-building of trainers and course managers, state-of-the-art training infrastructure, and industry-ready student evaluation system among others, would, more importantly, have positive employment outcomes of graduates from the vocational training system, especially in the existing industrial and economic scenarios where a considerably high demand for professional technicians exists.

Quality Concerns of ITI

The quality of India's vocational education and training (VET) system has been subject to considerable criticism in the past, which has also had an impact on the activities of foreign companies in India (Pilz and Li 2014). For example, in its Efficiency Study Report on Indian ITIs, the International Labour Organization (ILO) concluded that the employability of those completing training at state-run ITIs was poor and that only 30 to 40 percent found employment or became self-employed on completion of their training (ILO 2003, 31). The fact that the training provided does not match actual labor market demand has also drawn criticism. Each year, for example, those who graduate from ITIs include almost half the total number of welders, mechanics and electronic engineers who are already in employment in the Indian labor market.

A research report commissioned by Federation of Indian Chambers of Commerce and Industry (FICCI 2006) surveyed 69 ITIs and concluded that many lack the right technical equipment and that a shortage of funding means there is little scope for improvement. It also noted a shortage of trained instructors and few opportunities for in-service training.

A study by the National Skill Development Corporation of initial and continuing training for instructors (NSDC n.d.) found that most instructors at India's ITIs have received no pedagogical training and are not, therefore, adequately prepared to teach.

A more recent (2014) study of almost 150 state-run ITIs found that they were appropriately equipped (Joshi, Pandey, and Sahoo 2014, 95), but that there was a shortage of instructors, that instructors often lacked appropriate skills, and that many were employed on part-time or fixed-term contracts (105 ff.). It also found that more than 15 percent of all those who started training dropped out before completing the course (101) and that about a third were unemployed on completion of their training (103).

In a study of learning opportunities in fisher families in the state of Orissa, Pilz and Wilmshöfer (2015) found that ITIs were poorly equipped and that potential students had to travel long distances to access them. They also found a shortage of courses geared to the needs of students and the local employment market. Finally, research into street food vendors in two states also found that the formal training provision offered by ITIs did not meet the needs of potential trainees (Pilz, Uma, and Venkatram 2015). Given the vital importance of vocational training, it is surprising that there is so little by way of robust research findings in the area of quality.

A Study of Regular ITIs

Interviews were conducted in 2014 at state-run ITIs in the states of Karnataka, Orissa, and Tamil Nadu and in New Delhi; 15 case studies were investigated, representing different institution sizes and in both urban and rural settings. The aim of the study was not to reach generalizable conclusions about the quality of training at Indian ITIs but to make an initial exploratory contribution to fleshing out their concept of quality.

Defining Quality

The survey of principals showed that their understanding of quality is very strongly output-oriented. They regard employability and stakeholder satisfaction as the key markers of training quality, a view that reflects the requirements of the Indian government. Quality is associated with both output and income, that is, the skills and expertise acquired by trainees and opportunities available to them in the labor market, with a focus on the overlap between trainees' skills and the requirements of the labor market.

Our quality is measured by what our trainees have learned here, we focus on the output. When they get a job afterwards, then we know they had quality training. (ITI Karnataka)

The performance of our students is our indicator of quality—their practical and theoretical skills, as well as their behavior and way of thinking. (ITI Orissa)

In line with this definition of quality, the quality indicators used in the ITIs surveyed focus almost exclusively on using tests and examinations to assess trainees' knowledge. Other commonly cited indicators include employment rates on completion of training at an ITI, drop-out rates, and completion rates.

Assessing Quality

The input factors involved in quality of vocational training include instructors, infrastructure and equipment, and curriculum.

Most of the principals surveyed were satisfied with the training their instructors had, but some expressed concerns about their motivation, the currency of their knowledge, and the availability of adequate numbers of skilled instructors. In half the cases we investigated, principals were appointing external instructors on a temporary basis to fill vacancies. However, many reported that these temporary staff often lacked the necessary skills, so their appointment did not enhance training quality. To ensure the long-term teaching quality, they said it was important that instructors received regular in-service training and that both their technical knowledge and teaching methods were updated. There was little agreement, however, on the implementation of in-service training, suggesting that such training is inadequate and nonstandard.

It is essential that the trainers are well prepared, but not so much regarding what kind of diploma they have but if they can teach and motivate the students. (ITI Delhi)

They get a few days of training every three or four years, but only in technical aspects and not in teaching methods. (ITI Orissa)

Principals are of the opinion that the infrastructure and equipment of ITIs could be improved. In most cases, there is a shortage of machinery, tools, and space to teach modern technologies. There are also no regulations on maintaining machinery.

> I think we can be satisfied with what we have, compared to other institutions. But there is still a lot of room for improvement. (ITI Karnataka)

> We still require more machinery and updated technology. Therefore, we are not completely satisfied yet. (ITI Tamil Nadu)

Principals also addressed curriculum quality and were critical of the fact that curricula were extremely theoretical and bore no relation to practice or modern technologies.

> We are using the latest curriculum, but we are not satisfied with it. It is too vast, with too much theory and not enough practical parts. (ITI Tamil Nadu)

> We are not satisfied with the curriculum. It is not up to the modern standard, it just contains basic skill training. (ITI Delhi)

The ITIs surveyed placed particular emphasis on the smooth integration of trainees in the labor market, with a focus on positive outcomes. Some had a dedicated member of staff whose main role was to coordinate job placement. These placement officers maintain contacts with companies and act as the interface between potential employers and newly qualified trainees. ITIs also used alumni associations as networking platforms for former trainees.

> We have constant contact [with] industries. They come here and hire our students. We have a placement officer, who informs [us] about the openings and visits the companies. (ITI Orissa)

Potential for Quality Enhancement

Interviewees suggested ways of improving the quality of the training institutions. The key, they said, was to recruit enough skilled instructors. However, while higher salaries helped, the main obstacle was government constraints.

We require more manpower to improve the quality, but the government is not flexible enough to provide more staff. (ITI Tamil Nadu)

Interviewees also frequently referred in comments about equipment and infrastructure to the political and bureaucratic obstacles hampering their efforts to improve the situation.

A Study on Upgraded ITIs.   Toward producing technicians of world standard, the Government of India launched a program of upgrading 500 ITIs during 2005 to 2006 at the rate of 100 ITIs each year, and currently 1,896 government ITIs have been upgraded into so-called Centers of Excellence (COE) at the national level (Rao, Sahoo, and Ghosh 2014). Under this program appropriate infrastructure and equipment are provided. Furthermore, the program has the overall strategy of enlisting cooperation with Industry and Chamber of Commerce and to create a PPP model for designing and implementing the scheme. The salient features of the scheme of upgrading ITIs include the introduction of multiskilling courses of one-year duration followed by advanced/specialized modular courses through an industry-wise cluster approach with multi-entry and multi-exit provisions. Most of the ITIs impart training in engineering trades like instrument mechanic, electrician, fitter, plumber, diesel mechanic, computer operator and programming assistant (COPA), electrical mechanic, information technology, mechanic—computer hardware, refrigeration and air conditioning, turner, and welder. Establishing PPP in the form of IMCs is envisaged to ensure greater and active involvement of industry in various aspects of training.

A study has been launched to assess the progress of the program of COE in the South Indian state of Karnataka (Tara, Kumar, and Ramaswamy 2011). For the study purposes, 6 ITIs out of 36 ITIs upgraded to COEs formed the sample. The sample was chosen so as to provide regional representation, coverage of trade, and socioeconomic backwardness of the region. The main objective of the study was to assess the overall effectiveness of ITIs with respect to methods adopted for identification of trades that had industry demand (by way of discussions with industry representatives, IMC members, and ITI functionaries), existing infrastructure facilities, capacity of trainers, and curriculum development, among others. The principals and instructors of the sample ITIs were asked to give their opinions regarding the system of evaluation presently adopted and to offer suggestions for any modifications. As students are the critical elements of ITIs, a cross-section of students were interviewed to elicit their views about the program as well as the problems encountered by them. Furthermore, a cross-section of industry partners were interviewed to elicit their opinions with regard to the internship programs of ITIs, their role in teaching in the courses, training of instructors at ITIs by the industry experts, and so on.

The major findings of the study were the following:

- Although COE was a well-conceived program, lack of awareness regarding its uniqueness and usefulness among parents, students, and industry had resulted in very poor demand for the courses as the course had not achieved a brand image.
- While some of the sample COEs were endowed with adequate training infrastructure, including latest tools and equipment, there were others that lacked such training infrastructure. Interestingly, older COEs as compared to recent ones were relatively well-equipped in this regard. Most of the instructors reported that the training they had received was quite beneficial and stated that there was an urgent need for participating in such programs on a regular basis in order to keep pace with the latest advances in the industrial sectors. There were no career growth opportunities for the instructors, which was a demotivating factor.
- Findings regarding the status of girl students in the sample COEs indicate low intake of girls against sanctioned seats. Furthermore, the drop-out and pass rates also show a poor profile of girl students. For instance, in one of the sample COEs, though there was a sanctioned intake provision for 32 girl students, none were admitted during the reference period. In another sample COE, out of 11 girls who were admitted, 3 had dropped out and the other 8 failed. The findings clearly emphasize the urgent need for focusing on the girl students in the training transaction and placement activities, providing a conducive social ambience and extending support that would enhance their self-esteem and motivate them

to excel in their studies. Interestingly, women trainees are generally not preferred by the industry as the tasks involve handling of heavy material and equipment besides working in inconvenient shifts. Furthermore, women have to work in close proximity with boys/ men, which is culturally not acceptable.

- The role of the IMCs appeared to be weak in many sample COEs and limited to only a few issues such as financial approvals, procurement-related matters, and, to some extent, student placements. IMCs appeared to play only an advisory role without adequate powers and minimal roles in the areas of staff training, constant interaction with the industry to generate demand for COE students, instilling confidence among students through regular interaction, and providing all necessary support and guidance.

- The major problems experienced by students in the course of their study included comprehension difficulties due to poor English knowledge and communication skills, absence of, or inadequate, stipend, lack of hostel facilities, and inadequate transport facilities.

It is clear that the existing training courses offered through ITIs focus only on theory rather than practical components. In this context, it could also be said that the link between general and higher education is weak. It does not meet the future skill requirements of the labor market. It further complicates the transition from education into the labor market. Thus, the interaction with the labor market becomes clear. The labor market is characterized by a high degree of liberality in India. Flexibility and high turnover are two aspects that have been mentioned repeatedly in many studies. They make an extensive and, therefore, expensive company training to a high-risk investment because of the deferred migration risk. In addition, it is important to remember that in India, more than 90 percent of workers are allocated in the unorganized sector (Singh 2012, 181;). This means that there are no regulated working conditions (e.g., activities in small family businesses or as day laborers). A corollary is that only about 2 percent of the workforce has undergone any formal vocational qualification (Singh 2012, 181). As a consequence, it is clear that the employers seeking workers must either focus on a relatively small group of more theoretically qualified ITI graduates or on unskilled assistants who cannot accept challenging tasks.

Polytechnics

Polytechnic education in India contributes significantly to India's economic development. Most of them offer three-year generalized diploma courses in conventional disciplines such as civil, electrical, and mechanical engineering. During the past two decades many polytechnics started offering courses in other disciplines such as electronics, computer science, medical lab technology, hospital engineering, and architectural assistantship. In addition, many single-technology institutions are also offering diploma programs in areas like leather technology, sugar technology, and printing technology. Many diploma programs are also being offered exclusively for women in women's polytechnics, such as in garment technology, beauty culture and textile design. Polytechnics are meant to provide skills after class 10 and the duration of diploma programs is 3 years, which means the trainee becomes employable at the age of 19 years. Polytechnics are also offering postdiploma and advanced diploma programs of 12 years duration in different specializations. The aim of polytechnic education is to create a pool of skill-based manpower to support shop floor and field operations as a middle-level link between technicians and engineers. The pass-outs of diploma-level institutions in engineering and technology play an important role in managing shop floor operations. It is also an established fact that small- and medium-scale industries prefer to employ diploma holders because of their special skills in reading and interpreting drawings, estimating, costing and billing, supervision, measurement, testing, repair, maintenance, and so on.

Growth of Polytechnics in India

Type of institution	1990–1991	2003–2004(P)	2004–2005(P)	2005–2006(P)	2009–2010	2010–2011	2011–2012	2012–2013
Polytechnic institutes	879	1,105	1,171	1,274	2,324	3,254	3,428	3,524

Source: https://www.aicte-india.org/downloads/aph_nveqf_241212_final.pdf
P = *Provisional.*

During the past decade, India has seen a tremendous increase in the number of engineering colleges at degree level throughout the country. However, the growth of technical institutions has not been uniform as far as the number of polytechnics and graduate engineering colleges is concerned. The present student intake in degree and diploma-level technical institutions is 653,000 and 354,000, respectively. The ratio of degree to diploma holders is around 2:1, whereas ideally it should be 1:3. This is because of more private participation in the engineering sector compared to the diploma sector. There is also a societal perception that degrees command a premium in the job market compared to diplomas. A nation-wide scheme of "Sub-mission on Polytechnics" has also been launched. Under this scheme new polytechnics will be set up in every district not having one already. These polytechnics will be established with central funding and over 700 will be set up through PPP and private funding. All these new polytechnic institutes will have a community polytechnic wing. Women's hostels will also be set up in all the government polytechnics. The existing government polytechnics will be in incentivized to modernize in PPP mode. Efforts will also be made to increase intake capacity by using space, faculty, and other facilities in the existing polytechnics in shifts. There is also a shortage of qualified diploma holders in several new areas. Therefore, engineering institutions will be incentivized and encouraged to introduce diploma courses to augment intake capacity. Diploma programs could be run in evening shifts when the laboratory, workshop, equipment, and library are free.

Main Problems of Polytechnic Education in India

Over the years, the diploma programs have deteriorated losing the skill components, which has resulted in their being just a diluted version of degree education. The organizations employing them have to train them all over again in basic skills. Major problems being faced by the polytechnic education system are

1. nonavailability of courses in new and emerging areas
2. inadequate infrastructure facilities and obsolete equipment
3. system unable to attract quality teachers

4. inadequate financial resources
5. inadequate or nonexistent state policies for training and retraining of faculty and staff
6. lack of flexibility and autonomy to the institutions
7. inadequate industry–institute participation
8. lack of R&D in technician education
9. antiquated curricula.

Instructional Methods. The instructional strategy employed in polytechnics is predominately classroom-based teaching. Laboratory practices are conducted as per requirements in specific subjects. Many of the polytechnics have acquired adequate audiovisual hardware through special schemes of the central government. However, an adequate amount of courseware/software is not available, thus hampering the use of this media.

Equipment and Facilities. Many of the polytechnics were established about 30 years ago, and infrastructure in terms of buildings and equipment provided to the polytechnics at that time is still being used and has remained unchanged or has not been upgraded. Changes in technology and field practices call for corresponding changes in equipment and laboratory facilities. Due to resource constraints, most of the facilities have not been updated adequately. The Government of India has been providing grants under Direct Central Assistance to keep the polytechnics updated. The present World Bank–assisted project has the objective of modernizing the facilities, resources, and courses in polytechnics.

Community Polytechnics

The community polytechnics act as important centers for the application of science and technology in rural areas and generate self and wage-based employment opportunities, through nonformal training toward competency- and need-based courses in various trades and multiple skills. Community polytechnics have been established as entities within polytechnics rather than as autonomous institutions. This is because they are equipped with adequate infrastructure in the form of buildings, lecture halls, laboratories, workshop, and student hostels that connect them as centers of knowledge to the rural community. Besides, polytechnics have qualified and trained faculty, whose services could be utilized for vocational training and transfer of technology. To that extent, community polytechnics are part of the formal system. However, they provide training within communities, and their approach can be considered as informal. They deliver short-term courses of usually 6 months duration in various trades, free of any charges, and the intake of trainees is limited to 15 per cohort per trade. They also deliver training in collaboration with government departments and other agencies. The duration of such course is decided jointly by the departments and agencies. The community polytechnics design their own course curriculum. The scheme of Community Development through Polytechnics (CDTP) was initiated in the 10th Plan period and is presently mandated to continue till the end of 12th Plan period. Presently, there are 518 community polytechnics established in the country (http://mhrd.gov .in/technical-education-20).

The Scheme of Community Development through Polytechnics (CDTP)

In an increasingly competitive economic environment of our country, the unorganized sector, which is so important for the country, needs to increase the productivity of its manpower for its survival and growth. Yet another paradox before the Indian informal sector is that it cannot afford employing highly educated and professionally trained manpower who usually aspire for highly challenging, rewarding, and satisfying careers. The only option available before the Indian informal sector is to depend upon relatively low-paid manpower trained through nonformal system of skill development. There is, therefore, an urgent need to train millions of persons every year through a countrywide network of nonformal skill development. Such nonformal skill training should attract beneficiaries from all cross-sections of the Indian society with special emphasis on SCs/ STs, OBCs, women, school dropouts, minorities, physically disabled, economically weaker sections of the society, and other underprivileged persons. Technology divide is clearly visible in Indian urban and rural society. Vast majority of Indian urban population and a small fraction of those who live in rural areas and slums enjoy the benefits of modern technologies. Vast majority of rural people and those living in slums require assistance in adopting appropriate technology for benefitting from investment in science and technology and enhancing their productivity and standard of living. There is, therefore, an immediate need to evolve a vast network that can help in the adoption of appropriate technologies among rural people and slum dwellers. Sustainable use of technology by such people would involve technology demonstration, repair and maintenance services, counselling and consultancy services, and free service camps from time to time (Government of India, Department of Higher Education 2009).

There are more than 1,419 polytechnics and equivalent technical institutions that exhibit potential to provide skill training to millions of youth through their own facilities and by establishing extension centers in collaboration with ITIs, KVKs, vocational institutes and NGOs. These polytechnics can also render useful services in adopting appropriate technologies and providing technical and support services to rural people and slum dwellers. AICTE-approved polytechnics are considered to be a viable vehicle for providing the intended services as mentioned earlier. The rationale for choosing AICTE-approved polytechnics for the implementation of the Scheme of Community Development through polytechnics is based on the fact that AICTE-approved polytechnics are equipped with the following type of resources: (i) physical facilities in the form of buildings, lecture halls, laboratories, workshops, hostels, and so on that could be used as knowledge and skill centers for rural community and slums dwellers; (ii) qualified and trained faculty who can scientifically formulate, implement, and monitor community-oriented programs and projects, especially where the activity of adoption of appropriate technology is involved; (iii) technicians and craftsmen whose services can be utilized to some extent for imparting skill training and adoption of appropriate technologies; and (iv) students of polytechnics could be of tremendous help in making meaningful contribution to community and rural development. Polytechnics can, therefore, render vital assistance in community development work. This they can do partly by utilizing their own resources and partly by mobilizing the resources available at the higher technological institutions. The involvement of polytechnics in implementing the Scheme of Community Development through polytechnics is need of the hour.

The main objectives of the scheme are as follows:

- To carry out need assessment surveys to assess technology and training needs
- To impart skill development training to the intended target groups
- To disseminate appropriate technologies for productivity enhancement
- To provide technical and support services to rural masses and slums dwellers
- To create awareness among the target groups about technological advancement and contemporary issues of importance.

Need Assessment Survey

The identified polytechnics shall conduct the need assessment surveys of the area selected for activities. Such surveys should lead to determination of the felt needs and identification of the direction in which rural development efforts are likely to bring quicker results. Participatory rural appraisal/rapid rural appraisal (PRA/RRA) exercises can be conducted to understand socioeconomic and ecological condition of people and area to develop a micro-plan for selected villages. The identified institutions shall also make judicious use of comprehensive statistics already available from the Directorate of Economic and Statistics, Census Office functioning in each state/union territory, credit plans of the banks, studies conducted by NGOs, and so on. Based on the outcomes of these surveys, the identified polytechnics should prepare detailed, time-bound "Annual Operational Plan" indicating objectives, targets to be accomplished in measurable terms, resource needs, implementation processes, complete time schedule for each activity to attain the set objectives, and monitoring and evaluation mechanisms. The detailed plan (micro-plan) should also identify clearly the responsibilities and functions of all such governmental, nongovernmental, and grass-root agencies like village cooperatives and self-help groups (SHGs) whose involvement is considered necessary.

A suggestive list of need assessment surveys to be conducted is given in Annexure A. However, each polytechnic may carry out various surveys at their own level.

Skill Development Training Programs

In order that human resource is developed for gainful employment/self-employment, training must be need based and should provide employable/self-employable skills. The purpose of skill development is to create skilled and knowledge-based manpower by empowering students technically so that they can acquire sustainable livelihood. All training programs should be well-designed through graded exercises, keeping in view the market requirements for various trades. Short-term, nonformal, modular courses of 3 to 6 months duration, depending on the local needs and available local resources with proper structures having the desired flexibility to facilitate self-paced open learning mode (OLM), should be offered. Depending on local circumstances in some cases multiskill training may be offered to make self-employment viable in the rural economy. In some trades, advance skill course for 3 to 6 months duration may be designed and offered as per the interest of trainees or as per the demands of local companies/industries/market. Preferences may be given to the training courses with technical bias.

The objectives of skill development programs under CDTP are broadly as follows:

- Providing basic skills, knowledge, and attitudes for self-/wage employment to intended beneficiaries in their own villages/communities or nearby areas.
- Imparting entrepreneurial skills for initiating micro/tiny enterprises, especially for rural youth and community.
- Offering skill upgradation programs in their own fields or for adoption of appropriate technologies to enhance their employment prospects; for example, masons may be trained for construction of biogas plants, low-cost latrines, water storage tanks, ferro-cement articles, and blacksmith may be trained in welding, fabrication, and so on.

- Identifying and conducting special skill training programs for women, SCs/STs, OBCs, minorities, school dropouts, street children, physically handicapped, economically weaker sections of the society, and other underprivileged persons.
- Special training programs on health, hygiene, and sanitation and mechanization of sanitary services and skill programs pertaining to liberation and rehabilitation of scavengers may be organized.

Salient features desirable under skill development and training to be achieved in future are as follows:

- The skill development programs chosen for training shall be based on the findings of need assessment surveys and the felt need of the locality. A lot more emphasis needs to be given to devise strategies for meeting the growing demands of the service sector.
- Each identified polytechnic should conduct a survey for the identification of priority needs for skill training programs targeting a cluster of 10 to 20 villages every year. DRDA, NGOs, voluntary agencies, village panchayats, and retired teachers, engineers, and other reputed persons should be involved in the process.
- The skill programs offered should be flexible and nonformal with open access to all, without any preconditions based on age, sex, and educational qualifications.
- The identified polytechnics should target the poor and deprived sections of the society in both urban and rural areas, specifically women, SCs/STs, OBCs, minorities, school dropouts, street children, physically handicapped, economically weaker sections of the society, and other underprivileged persons.
- To facilitate self-employment in the service sector, emphasis should be on multiskill training, whereas for employment in production centers, training may be given either on specialized designated skills or multitrade skills depending on the needs and requirements of target population.
- Possibility of sharing of financial/infrastructural/skill resources available with different institutions/organizations/agencies may be explored.

- Infrastructure available in polytechnics should be utilized in conducting various training programs.
- Infrastructure available in ITIs/vocational schools/colleges/technical institutions wherever available may be utilized for skill development programs.
- Trainees may be rewarded with certificates for the competencies they have developed, indicating the level of proficiency attained through participation in skill development programs. Such certificates issued by polytechnics will help employing agencies with the recruitment processes.
- The identified polytechnics may collaborate with potential employers in their vicinity to award certificates jointly to the participants of skill development programs.
- The identified polytechnics should develop a proper feedback mechanism to know the posttraining status of trainees specifically with regard to their getting self-/wage employment.
- The major criteria for judging the effectiveness of training imparted are rate of employability and skills attained by trainees. Polytechnics should provide only need-based skill development programs.

Dissemination and Application of Appropriate Technologies

A large number of technologies have been developed by various research institutions and laboratories in the form of appropriate technologies. However, benefits of these technologies have failed to reach the rural population. Villagers could not adopt these modern technologies to improve productivity and, in turn, quality of life, since technology transfer did not take place in a planned manner. It is in this context that the identified polytechnics need to play a significant role in this important task. This may be done systematically by carrying out the following:

- Collecting details of all available appropriate technologies from various agencies and organizations engaged in the research and development of appropriate technologies through National Institute of Technical Teachers Training and Research (NITTTR) and by other means, adapting them to suit local conditions with regular and relevant feedback from Extension Centers, and, disseminating, through field demonstrations, these technologies in villages and, thus, helping villagers to appreciate and adopt technological innovations.

- Creating awareness among villagers about advancements in science and technology that are relevant to them and educating, training, and motivating them in acquiring skills required to use those technologies as well as technologies in different fields such as rural water supply, sanitation, shelter, habitat, communication, transportation, agriculture, agro-based food technology, nonconventional sources of energy for rural areas, construction, service sector, and so on.
- Helping villagers through technical support services, to install, maintain, and sustain appropriate technologies like agriculture implements, energy devices, rural water- and sanitation-based technologies, rainwater harvesting structures, rural housing, suitable local transportation, and sustainable agriculture.
- Developing innovative strategies for mass involvement of rural people to transfer and sustain technologies.
- Assisting in the establishment of display-cum-demonstration centers in villages so that awareness about appropriate technologies can be created.

Introducing Modern Gadgets and Machinery for Generating Employment in Rural Areas

- To achieve the targets and accelerate activities in the dissemination and application of technology, the following points are to be taken into consideration while implementing the Scheme of Community Development through polytechnics.
- Identify location-specific proven technologies, and this in turn should be transferred to villages in a targeted manner. The basic deciding parameters for an appropriate technology or any rural development projects are as follows. The technology should be (a) socially acceptable, (b) economically feasible, (c) technically practical, and (d) environment-friendly.
- Need-based and community-friendly technologies are essential because traditional technologies are not always competitive and

may not generate enough local employment for the livelihood. The vast informal sector needs introduction of new and improved technologies and upgradation of skills of its manpower and other inputs.

- Transfer of appropriate and latest technologies to rural people to improve their productivity, efficiency, and quality of life, offering, where needed, upgradation of existing technologies used by artisans and villagers.

- The transfer of technology is not simply transfer of knowledge and skill for producing some products. It entails need analysis, technology identification, design, fabrication, development, testing, application, production, marketing, management, and maintenance. It needs a proper delivery system and a strong component of demand and employment generation.

- Providing backup technical support to the panchayat, Zilla Parishad, NGOs, and grassroots community at large is expected to bear fruits to a certain extent.

- Marketing of rural produce and products can be carried out through different activities, such as holding exhibitions or fairs like Gram Shree Mela and Kisan Mela, to promote the sale of produce and products of farmers/rural artisans. Sale of handicrafts, organic food, herbal products/alternative medicines, and so on has been increasing rapidly in the global market. Therefore, polytechnics can help with developing a retail marketing network and organizing small cooperatives to support rural artisans and small farmers.

- Polytechnics should intensify their interaction with National Institutes of Technical Teachers Training and Research (NITTTR) and different research institutions/laboratories to accelerate the use of technology in villages.

- NITTTRs may make efforts to identify more technologies and help polytechnics apply them to benefit the community. To boost application of appropriate technology, a "Technology Demonstration and Dissemination Centre" may be set up at each NITTTR.

Technical and Support Services

In rural areas, a large number of equipment are used in both farm and nonfarm sectors. For their sustained working, proper repair and maintenance services are to be provided. The identified polytechnic should help villagers and other agencies to take up this work by organizing the following:

- Minor repairs of equipment through extension centers and also at site
- Service centers to serve a cluster of villages
- Promotion of service centers and repair shops to be set up by villagers themselves
- Technical service camps in villages at regular intervals
- Extending consultancy services at the village level using trained manpower.

Creating Awareness among the Target Groups about Technological Advancement and Contemporary Issues of Importance

Assimilation and dissemination of information on rural development is another important activity. Information, education, and communication (IEC) plays a vital role in changing the attitudes of villagers for adopting a better lifestyle and technologies. This can be done through publication and distribution of technical literatures containing information useful to the rural people. For this purpose, all communication media such as leaflets, brochures, filmstrips, and video films and other audiovisual aids are to be used. To promote these activities, the following approaches can be adopted:

- Dissemination of information to end-users and others may be made through various media. Modern as well as folk media (like puppet show, *nukkad-natak*, *nautanki*, etc.) should be effectively used for creating awareness among masses.
- Providing information through exhibitions at village extension centers.

- Organizing youth clubs, Mahila Mandal (women's club), farmers' clubs, and so on.
- Organizing special exhibitions, community workshops, group discussions, seminars, and so on in villages.
- Using mass media like video films, films, radio, and television networks.
- Organizing technical camps, demonstration camps, mobile exhibitions, and so on.
- Putting up hoardings and display boards at appropriate public places.
- Releasing advertisements on regular basis.

Community College

The community college is an alternative system of education that is aimed at the empowerment of the disadvantaged and the underprivileged (urban poor, rural poor, tribal poor, and women) through appropriate skills development leading to gainful employment in collaboration with the local industry and the community and achieve skills for employment and self-employability of the above sections of people in the society. It is an innovative educational alternative rooted in the community that aims to provide holistic education to the rural population and make them eligible for employment.

The vision of the community college is to be "of the Community, for the Community and by the Community" and to produce responsible citizens. Community colleges keep the community engaged with the affairs of the colleges in several formal and informal ways. Community is represented on the academic and administrative bodies of these colleges. Community colleges often have multiple campuses underlying the principle to set up the learning facility at a location that is not more than a 30-minute drive from any point, thereby making education accessible and affordable. These colleges give preference for admission to the local community, particularly, the marginalized sections of population that include minorities (non-White race/ethnicity), uneducated (first-generation degree seekers), backward areas (domicile), and those hailing from low-income background. Strong college–industry interaction leads to regular updating of curricula.

Skill-based courses are essentially about providing "hands-on" practice and experience (http://mhrd.gov.in/community-colleges). Community college promotes job-oriented, work-related, skill-based, and life-coping education. Its initiatives align with the Indian political will that prioritizes in education, primary education, information technology education, and vocational education. The key operating words in understanding the community college system are access, flexibility in curriculum and teaching methodology, cost-effectiveness, and equal opportunity in collaboration with industrial, commercial, and service sectors of the local area and responding to the social needs and issues of the local community, internship and job placement within the local area, promotion of self-employment and small business development, and declaration of competence and eligibility for employment. Lack of recognition has been a major problem faced by those who passed out from the community colleges, indicating difficulties in getting employment. Another important problem that community colleges face today is financial viability. Fees collected from students are very low (on average Rs.2,500 to 3,000); the low-fee structure is retained to make the system cost-effective and affordable to the poor and the most disadvantaged (Planning Commission 2003).

Jan Shikshan Sansthans (JSS)

New employment opportunities in industrial establishments could absorb only persons with required skills, and those rejected for the lack of required skills formed a large chunk of population. Even though they were skilled in their own way, that is, agricultural activities, they were not skilled in industrial operations. This created a unique situation in which they were not only problem to themselves but also to city dwellers, as these were mostly adults and young persons in search of employment but could not get jobs for want of proper skills. This drew the attention of administrators and policymakers.

Hence, Shramik Vidyapeeth, an institution for skill development, was set up to impart specialized education integrated with awareness and functional improvement for such people. In the context of the country's overall development, this program was conceived in order to meet the educational and vocational needs of numerous groups of adults and young people;

these groups comprised men and women belonging mostly to the unorganized, urban informal sector, living and working in urban and industrial areas, and people migrating from rural to urban settings who were expected to derive substantial benefits from skill development centers.

The first Shramik Vidyapeeth was established in Worli, Mumbai, in March 1967 under the aegis of Bombay City Social Education Committee, a voluntary organization engaged in adult education for decades. Encouraged by the successful functioning of this Shramik Vidyapeeth, the Government of India gradually expanded the scheme to other parts of the country. In the year 2000 the name of the institution was changed as Jan Shikshan Sansthan (JSS) with an enhanced role in the area of adult and lifelong education. Today, there are 271 JSSs located in 27 states and 2 union territories. They impart training in various skills and cover on an average 500,000 to 600,000 beneficiaries every year. The expansion of the number of JSSs in different Five Year Plans is given in the following table:

Plan period	Number of JSS sanctioned	Total
Up to 7th Plan period	58	58
9th Plan	50	108
10th Plan	90	198
11th Plan	73	271

These institutions are nonformal adult education institutions that impart literacy-linked vocational courses. They offer training in a number of vocational courses with varying durations to different clientele. In view of the inherent strength of these institutions in the field of vocational education and training, they have become more popular and are in demand by nongovernment organizations. Some of the strong points of Sansthans are detailed as follows:

A) A JSS is a registered organization under the Societies Registration Act with its own Memorandum of Association and Rules and Regulations and also run under the aegis of an NGO. Hence, it has autonomy in running the institution and organizing programs. The management of the Sansthan is with a board of management that is represented by both nonofficial and official members.

B) The Sansthans are fully funded by the National Literacy Mission Authority (NLMA), Ministry of Human Resource Development, Government of India. The annual recurring lump-sum grant is released to meet the expenditures under three heads: emoluments, office expenditures, and programs.

C) The programs are organized based on the need of the clientele. Hence, the number of courses organized is more. Need assessment is done through surveys.

D) The clientele include neoliterates, illiterates, and people with rudimentary level of education.

E) Practical work (hands-on) is given priority in training programs. As a result, the performance of trainees on the job is far better than others who undergo training in both formal or informal systems. Out of the total duration of training programs, 65 percent is earmarked for practical, 25 percent for theory, and 10 percent for life enrichment education.

F) The curriculum, lesson plan, and teaching–learning materials are developed by the Sansthans.

G) Locally available trained manpower is engaged as resource persons for different skill development programs. This enables the trainers to have an immediate connect to the trainees.

H) As the district is the operational area of the Sansthan and the demand for skill training is from all over the district, training programs are organized in collaboration with other agencies/departments. Collaboration includes use of physical facilities, equipment, financial help, and so on.

I) The learner achievement is tested more by practical work. Persons who are not literate are given freedom to face viva voce to complete the test in theory.

After the launch of Saakshar Bharat program, the JSSs are expected to play a major role in the area of skill development. They will be institutionally networked with the adult education centers so that they impart skill development training as well as literacy-linked vocational training. The Sansthans, in coordination with the district implementing agency will enlist neoliterates for appropriate skill development training. Hence, they have to necessarily gear themselves to apply total quality management (TQM) principles. They have to make drastic shift from the current mode of conventional working to a more innovative one to adapt themselves to the changing demands of the country's industry and economy. This is borne out through various evaluation studies of the Sansthans as well as the scheme itself.

In order to enable JSSs to play their role properly in Saakshar Bharat a number of new initiatives have been taken up by the National Literacy Mission Authority/ Directorate of Adult Education in recent times. They include:

1. Standardized curriculum:
    From the year 2011 to 2012 onwards, JSSs are directed to conduct skill training programs only based on standardized curriculum that is approved by competent institution/agency. In this regard, Sansthans are directed to use the curriculum already standardized by the Directorate of Adult Education for 36 vocational courses and by National Institute of Fashion Technology (NIFT) for 23 courses.

    Action has also been taken to standardize the course curriculum of vocational courses conducted by Sansthans with help from other professional institutions like National Institute of Open Schooling (NIOS) and Indira Gandhi National Open University (IGNOU).

2. Use of ICT:
    In order to stimulate learners' interest, improve the learning process, and enhance the learning ability of beneficiaries, use of ICT has been given priority. In this regard computerized vocational training modules have been developed with the help of Amrita University for courses on plumbing and fabric painting, which are reported to have high success rate during field-testing. More such modules are being developed for use in training programs.

3. Standardization of cost estimates:
    Cost estimate of different vocational courses conducted by Sansthans have been standardized in the regional workshops. Costs differ from one region to the other.

4. Standardized format for annual action plan:

   The format for submission of annual action plan has been designed in excel sheet giving all the details, including duration of courses, number of beneficiaries, honorarium for resource persons, cost of T/L materials, per-trainee cost, and so on.

   The draft action plans are now being reviewed by peer groups comprising of selected directors of state resource centers (SRCs), JSSs, and technical experts.

5. Web-based monitoring system:

   Web-based management and monitoring system has been developed with the help of National Informatics Centre (NIC). The JSS portal provides an interface to accept annual action plans online with a provision to approve, modify, or reject plans along with remarks. Through this portal, details such as progress in the implementation of planned programs, income and expenditure, and beneficiaries covered are reviewed.

6. Assessment and certification:

   Action has been initiated to conduct the assessment test and certification of the beneficiaries of Sansthans by professional organizations like NIFT, NIOS, and IGNOU.

7. Impact evaluation:

   Evaluation is an audit and appraisal of the program outcomes in terms of qualitative and quantitative dimensions of pace and impact of the skill development training. Every JSS is evaluated once in 3 years by an external agency empanelled with National Literacy Mission Authority. In the recent past, 150 JSSs have been evaluated in 7 batches and evaluation of 136 Sansthans is ongoing.

8. Performance audit:

   The performance audit of JSSs has been done in Madhya Pradesh with the help of reputed agencies like Institute of Public Audit of India (IPAI), Financial Management Research and Resource Society (FMRRS), and Centre for Social and Management Solutions (CSMS) to assess performance and fund utilization. Similar such exercise will be carried out for other Sansthans also.

9. Capacity building of the staff:

As part of capacity building, directors of JSSs are invited to attend various meetings/workshops/orientation programs in connection with vocational education and Saakshar Bharat. Separate provision has been made in the budget for capacity building of the staff of JSSs. It is also proposed to involve reputed national and international agencies in capacity building of not only the staff of the Sansthans but also the resource persons.

10. Release of funds:

To receive grants from the government, JSSs are required to submit an affidavit regarding coverage of beneficiaries as per the policies of the scheme, constitution/reconstitution of the board of management, appointment of regular director, and nominal fee charged. The second installment is released only on the basis of performance and expenditure incurred.

Follow-up meetings are conducted to review the progress made in the selection of products and loan sanctioned to ST beneficiaries.

A lot of action is still needed in future to improve the total quality management (TQM), which includes the following:

A) Assessing the demand for skills developed and establishing tie-ups with marketing avenues to promote the sale of beneficiaries' products and services
B) Training in soft skills and marketing strategies to be provided to beneficiaries to enable them to become skilled entrepreneurs
C) Train beneficiaries to interact meaningfully with customers and other agencies during posttraining activities
D) Close monitoring and supervision of training programs
E) QA of products crafted by trainees for better marketing
F) Infusion of professionalism into all aspects.

The authors have conducted several studies to evaluate the functioning of JSSs and also carried out a nation-level evaluation of the effectiveness of activities of JSS, and the studies revealed the following major challenges encountered by JSSs:

1. Extremely poor infrastructure both at the office premises and in the outside centers in a significantly high percentage of JSSs across the country.

2. Lack of adequate funds and poor flow of the meager grant amount.

3. In most cases, the JSS does not have a repository of resource persons. Even if they do, they cannot afford to utilize their services as the honorarium they can pay is very meager and do not meet even the travel expenses of the resource persons.

4. The syllabi for various vocational courses are prepared by the respective JSS with the help of their vocational resources persons who are not experts in preparing syllabi that align with the latest developments in the field. No experts are involved in this exercise. The curricula for 36 courses are given by Directorate of Adult Education and not updated periodically with the help of end-users.

5. JSS certificates are not given recognition by most states, even by their respective employment exchanges.

6. The poor convergence between JSS, SRC, and Zilla Saksharatha Samithi (ZSS) is a matter of great concern. Convergence with other departments is also equally important for the functioning of JSS.

7. Lack of focus on the quality of training as well as the quality of products and services of beneficiaries is another vital area that has not received its due emphasis. Lack of professionalism in QA is a major deterrent in the scheme.

Financing Skill Development

Budget allocations by the MSDE over the years indicate a steady increase in funding provided for skill development and also point to the priority given to this sector of development. Government has sharply increased the allocation of funds and resources to support skill development efforts. The MSDE's actual expenditure in 2016 to 2017 stood at Rs.2,173 crore (revised estimates, and 1 crore = 10 million). This amount was increased in the 2017–2018 budget to Rs.3,016 crore.

Revised Estimates 2016–2017 (Figures in crores)			Revised Estimates 2017–2018 (Figures in crores)		
Revenue	Capital	Total	Revenue	Capital	Total
2,151.04	21.96	2,173.00	2,766.11	250.03	3,016.14

Source: http://www.domain-b.com/economy/budget/union_budget_2017/

The skill development programs of other union ministries have also benefitted. The budget proposed to increase allocations for Deendayal Antyodaya Yojana—National Rural Livelihood Mission for the promotion of skill development and livelihood opportunities for people in rural areas to Rs.4,500 crore in 2017 to 2018. Besides imparting new skills to the people in rural areas, mason training will be provided to 0.5 million people by 2022, with an immediate target of training at least 20,000 people by the end of financial year 2017 to 2018.

Pradhan Mantri Kaushal Kendras have already been promoted in over 60 districts, and the budget now proposes to extend these Kendras to more than 600 districts across the country. The government also aims to establish a 100 India International Skills Centers across the country. These centers would offer advanced training and courses in foreign languages, which are supposed to "help those of our youth who seek job opportunities outside the country."

In 2017 to 2018, the budget also proposed to launch the Skill Acquisition and Knowledge Awareness for Livelihood Promotion program (SANKALP) at a cost of Rs.4,000 crore, with the aim to provide market-relevant training to 30.5 million youth.

The next phase of "skill strengthening for industrial value enhancement" will also be launched in 2017 to 2018 at a cost of Rs.2,200 crore, a program that will focus on improving the quality and market relevance of vocational training provided in ITIs and strengthen the apprenticeship programs through an industry-cluster approach.

The 2017 budget reinforced the idea that government seems to believe that India's skill development challenge can essentially be met by government efforts. Less than 5 percent of India's workforce of 500 million has received any form of formal vocational training. Moreover, half of our workforce in 2010 was either illiterate or had primary/less than primary education. Hence, apart from education for all, skill development has also become a huge challenge. Given these twin challenges and that we are now adding some 5 to 7 million youth to the labor force annually—not 12 million as is commonly believed—who have higher levels of education than those currently in the labor force, it is critical that government's own education efforts must ensure that all children are completing 8 years of schooling and that actual learning in school is increased. In addition, given that governments, both union territories and states, have limited financial resources, the central government should not be increasing financial allocation to education and skill development simultaneously. In fact, the Union Budget of 2017 to 2018 is characterized by almost no efforts to increase allocation to education, which is unfortunate.

Clearly, government's own skills programs will grow as a result. However, this ignores the overwhelming evidence from around the world that no country that runs a government-driven system for technical and vocational education and training (TVET) has been successful in doing so. Government-driven systems are supply-driven, without regard to skill demands. Government-driven systems also tend to be financed by governments rather than those who will benefit most from the skill development—the employers and trainees. A recent World Bank study of the employment status of five government-financed programs states that only 27 percent of those who were a part of it received employment.

If TVET systems are employer-driven, they will be very responsive to demand and the changing needs of industry. However, the catch is that in order to be successful, employer-driven systems must also be employer-financed. As many as 63 countries, including those in Asia, Latin America, Europe, and Africa, have employer-financed and industry-driven systems.

Nevertheless, government-driven systems are rarely able to respond to the fast-changing technologies commensurate with market demand. This is not to say that government financing is not needed. It is needed so that the needs of the unorganized sector for skill development as well as the needs of the less privileged sections of youth are met. For the unorganized sectors, government-driven systems' role should be to ensure recognition of prior learning for those in the workforce, who, over the years, have acquired vocational skills on the job but have no certificate to prove it.

The government's financing and regulatory roles should be limited to these tasks. If it focuses on financing and providing skills to both organized and unorganized sectors along with performing a regulatory function, there will likely be a decline in the level of efficiency, effectiveness, and quality of training. However, the Union Budget is still reflective of a half-century-old philosophy of manpower planning—and financing such planning—with little regard to whether any of these trained youth get employment (Mehrotra 2014b).

According to 12th Plan Document of the Planning Commission, 85 percent of the labor force in India have educational qualification up to secondary level, within which 55 percent have an educational qualification only up to the primary level and merely 2 percent of its workforce have any vocational training. The government along with other agencies is trying to incentivize the students to encourage them to enroll in higher education and vocational training programs to keep pace with the increase in demand for skilled labor.

The low level of general education corresponds to the continuing high share of those engaged in agriculture and an even higher share of the total population that lives in rural areas. Economic growth should entail a transition of labor out of agriculture into manufacturing, nonmanufacturing industry, and services (Mehrotra et al. 2012). Low levels of education in the labor force, especially among those engaged in agriculture, make it more difficult for the latter to move into activities in urban areas; at best, they work as laborers in the construction industry. The low level of general education also makes it more difficult to provide vocational training to youth who have not even completed elementary education (i.e., until class 8). In other words, the first challenge for skill development in the 12th Plan is two-fold. The first is that government must ensure the existing 228 million workforce, 50 percent of whom are either illiterate or have only primary education or even less (these are likely to be functionally illiterate except for the ability to write their name), must achieve functional literacy and numeracy. Even though such workers have acquired their skills informally, they should be able to now get recognition of their prior learned skills on the basis of provisions in the National Skill Qualification Framework (NSQF) that recognize such skills. The second challenge is to ensure that all children between the ages of 6 and 14 are completing elementary education by the end of the 12th Plan, as required by the Right to Education Act, 2009. It is difficult to prepare a teenager for a vocation if they have not completed at least 8 years of schooling.

In the 11th Plan it was stated (based on National Sample Survey [NSS], 61st Round, 2004 to 2005) that among persons in the age range between 15 and 29 years, only about 2 percent are reported to have received formal vocational training and another 8 percent informal vocational training. These numbers (2 percent formally and 8 percent informally trained) refer to those who have received training and are in the labor force. However, using NSS 66th Round (2009 to 2010 data), we have estimated the stock of those who have received vocational training, formal or informal, or are receiving formal vocational training. In other words, our estimate of the vocationally trained refers not merely to those who are between 15 and 29 years of age (as shown in the 11th Plan) but also includes those between the ages 29 and 59; in other words, it covers the entire working-age group of 15 to 59 years in the labor force.

The absolute number of those receiving formal vocational training is 1.9 million in 2009–2010. An additional 9 million in the labor force have already received vocational training formally. Finally, an additional 32.7 million have received nonformal vocational training. Thus, the total number of those who received or were receiving vocational training in the labor force (aged between 15 and 59 years) in the 2009 to 2010 period was 43 million. In other words, only 10 percent of the labor force and workforce in the working-age group are vocationally trained (including those receiving training or completed their training) in 2009 to 2010.

Budget allocations for skill development programs

	Budget Estimates 2016–2017			Actual Expenditure 2016–2017		
	Plan	Non-Plan	Total	Plan	Non-Plan	Total
MSDE	1,425	41	1,466	710.35	19.33	729.68
DGT	275	63.28	338.28	154.83	71.23	226.06
Total	1,700	104.28	1,804.28	865.18	90.56	955.74

Note: MSDE—Ministry of Skill Development and Entrepreneurship; DGT—Director General Training.
Source: Government of India, Ministry of Skill Development and Entrepreneurship, Annual Report, 2016–2017.

CHAPTER 3

Addressing and Accomplishing Quality

The concept of quality management implies creating a set of policies and actions that facilitate the mobilization of the Industrial Training Institutes (ITIs) toward a quality culture that goes beyond mere certification. It implies a commitment to a new way of doing things in order to achieve objectives *from the beginning*. This commitment involves the whole organization. The quality problem stems out of the twin dimensions: (a) those trained but do not possess competencies for employability (either core or soft skills) and (b) mismatch between what is demanded and the skills supplied (Mehrotra 2014a).

It is interesting to note that several attempts are being made to accomplish quality standards through the establishment of National Vocational Quality Framework (NVQF) and Quality Council of India (QCI) among others. Furthermore, the industry has partnered with the government through National Skill Development Corporation (NSDC) and Sector Skill Councils (SSCs). With the help of industry, 33 SSCs have developed 1,661 Qualification Packs (QPs) covering 4,420 unique National Occupation Standards (NOSs). The industry is thus being roped in to help in creating curriculum, training the trainers, and, most importantly, supporting apprenticeship in the country. However, there has been some reluctance from the industry in providing a wage differential for skilled workers, leading to low absorption of skilled manpower. The industry needs to be educated on the benefits of employing a skilled workforce and the difference that skilled workers bring in terms of productivity and efficiency versus an unskilled worker (Interview with Sri S. Ramadorai, former president of NSDC, Government of India in Tara & Sanath Kumar, Skill Development in India, *IIMB Management Review*, 2016).

In order to address the growing international demands, national education and training systems are required to (a) adopt a broader mandate, (b) have a global vision, and (c) act locally. This will entail stronger alliances and increased cooperation with various stakeholders, including governmental institutions, vocational education and training (VET) providers and their staff, employers' associations, and trade unions. However, many countries have separate education systems and training systems that for generations have operated in relative isolation from one another. There are wide variations between the two sectors in terms of (a) their different cultures, governance, finance, and accountability, and (b) their standards, expectations, and ways of measuring learners' progress. There is a growing movement globally to adopt quality-focused VET strategies that rely on strong partnerships with stakeholders in order to make data-informed decisions about identified needs and expectations (Galvão 2014).

When vocational education provided in Germany is taken into consideration, the very system VET is given highest importance and is highly evolved. According to Sondermann (Ministerial Director, Head of Vocational Training Directorate),

> the vocational education and training system in Germany imparts high quality occupational competencies and vocational qualifications. High transition rates into labor market and low youth unemployment by international comparison underscore the significance of the vocational education of the German employment system.

According to Dr. Scheffler (Ministerial Director, Chair of Vocational Education Subcommittee), "the development of a European and, subsequently, a German qualification framework is an essential foundation if cooperation in the field of vocational education up to the year 2020 is to be based on reliable instruments." Since India has developed a National Vocational Qualification Framework (NVQF), it would be most ideal for Indian and German partners to work together to establish quality standards of vocational education being offered, especially in ITIs as the students transition into the world of work. This implementation of total quality management (TQM) in voice of customer (VOC), especially in an internationally competitive training environment, can provide a comparative advantage in preparing the quality workforce required for micro- and macroeconomic reforms. Quality-driven vocational training institutions will foster innovation and improvement and, thus, can have a strategic advantage in providing high-quality training.

Ensuring Quality in Delivery

There is a need for an independent system to assess quality, comprising all elements of the skill development value chain, right from need assessment and student mobilization up to training and placement. Current systems are primarily oriented toward quality checks (through trade tests) during the phase of assessment and certification.

We observe the need for the following:

- Quality frameworks, processes, and standards comprising of all elements of the skill development value chain
- A periodic quality assessment of training providers, be they public or private
- A plan to consistently improve performance (based on the results of periodic evaluation)
- A means to link funding to outcomes, once sufficient effort has been expended into taking steps to enhance quality and after adequate course-correction (i.e., after giving sufficient opportunity and support to training providers)
- A framework for incentivizing good performance.

The following is an illustrative framework for performance measurement and outcome-based funding.

What are the prime drivers of quality, especially in a program that aims to impart formal skill training of high professional standards? Quality will have to be driven (as well as be determined) by the following dimensions at the level of each/individual institute/center: (a) strong governance and administration, (b) adequate and appropriate faculty,

Assess	Improve	Measure	Fund
Understand unique feature pertinent to the institution	Benchmark against good practices in other institutes	Measure/monitor performance	Give sufficient time for vacational Training and skill development programs to reinvent and reorient themselves
Understand past performance capacity utilization, pass percentage, dropout rates and reasons for the same	Propose suitable ways to improve performance	Education process and practices	Additional funding based on performance and higher demand
	Changes pertaining to people (roles), process, and technology	Network with industry	
		Involving industry inferface bodies	Transfer of credits in student courses for optimal distribution
	Release initial funds for implementation	Placement, passouts, dropouts, and utilization rates	Funding based on measured outcomes
		Teacher quality and retention	

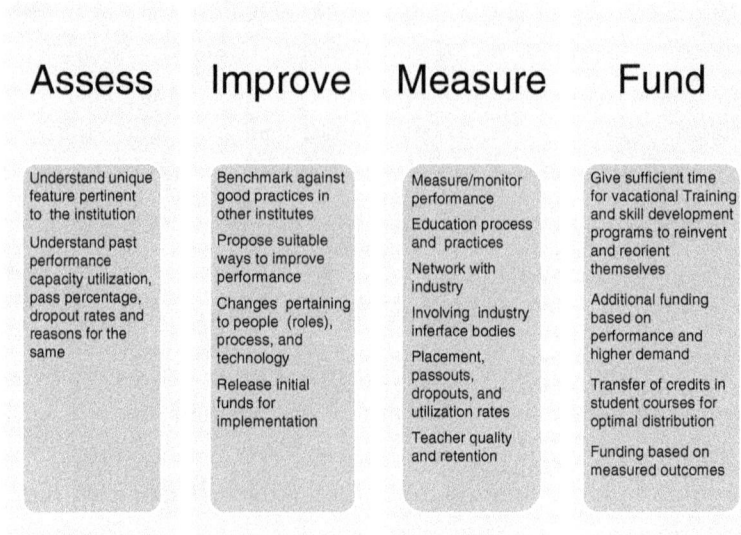

(c) current curriculum, (d) relevant infrastructure, and (e) a defined process for evaluation of student learning from in-gate to out-gate, employment, and employability that rewards partnerships.

Considering the magnitude of the challenge of skilling about 15 million persons every year and ensuring that the workforce of 500 million is adequately skilled by 2022, the way forward must comprise adequate initiatives to achieve these humungous targets in the right "scale" and "speed."

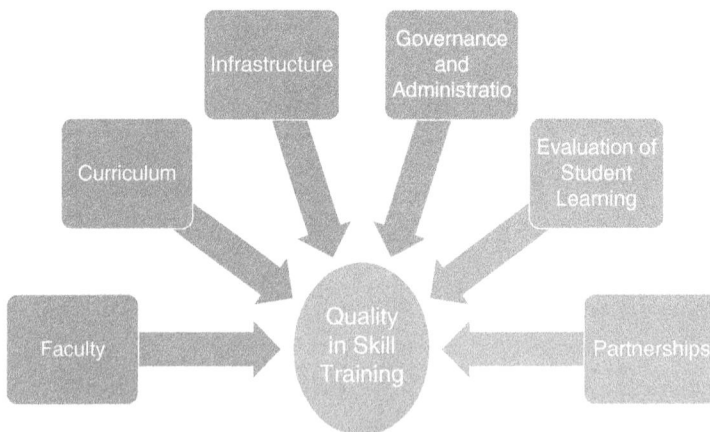

Determinants of quality in skills training

Some of the possible solutions to address the issues outlined are as follows:

- *Vocational education in schools should be enhanced.* This will present a channel for students to acquire skills, both life skills and industry-specific skills, during schooling. The vocational education system should be enhanced from the current 320,000 available under the National Institute of Open Schooling.
- *Creating a large talent pool through modular employable scheme (MES).* The MES framework provides a means for multiple-entry and multiple-exit skill development. It brings with it a flexibility to offer short-term, demand-led courses with partnerships. Increased adoption and will help achieve the required scale in skill development.
- *Targeting skill development at all levels of the "skill pyramid."* It is required to not only skill and educate the workforce to develop higher-level skills (which is key to ensuring industry competitiveness through research and intellectual property (IP), etc.) but also to adequately skill the workforce at the lower levels (i.e., where much of the workforce is concentrated).
- *Creating a large talent pool through MES*: The MES framework provides a means for multiple-entry and multiple-exit skill development. It brings with it a flexibility to offer short-term, demand-led courses with partnerships. Increased adoption and a stronger will would help achieve the required scale in skill development.

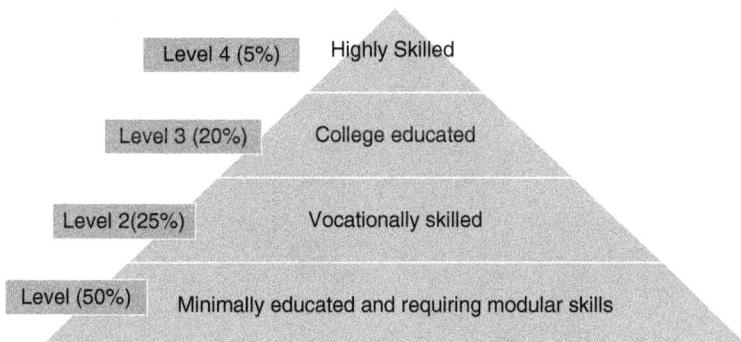

Level 4 (5%) — Highly Skilled

Level 3 (20%) — College educated

Level 2(25%) — Vocationally skilled

Level (50%) — Minimally educated and requiring modular skills

Targeting skill development at all levels of the "skill pyramid"

- *Formulation of institutional mechanisms for content formation, delivery, and assessment:* As demand for training grows, there will also be a cascading impact on the demand for content, standardized processes for training delivery, and uniform assessment practices. These will drive the demand for trainers and assessors, which will be a critical bottleneck as other pieces of the ecosystem fall in place. Furthermore, there would be a need for standards and quality processes (quality systems formulation, quality assessment, quality certification/training process certification) as the demand for training grows rapidly. These would require introducing institutional mechanisms specifying quality standards and practices.

- *Expediting the formulation of SSCs.* Given the need to ensure standards, industry involvement, and industry-led initiatives, what is required is to expedite the formulation of SSCs. The National Skill Development Policy has proposed the following roles for SSCs: identification of skill development needs; development of a sector skill development plan and maintaining skill inventory; determining skills/competency standards and qualifications; participation in affiliation, accreditation, examination, and certification processes; planning and executing the training of trainers; and promotion of academies of excellence.

- *Setting up a national human resource market information system (a national skill exchange).* The requirement for an information and communication technology (ICT)–enabled market information system will help both employers and employees provide details on specific demand as well as where does access to skilled workforce exists. This should not be limited just to the vocationally skilled workforce but also be made available to those seeking higher-level skills.

CHAPTER 4

Integrating Traditional Family-based Skills and Vocations—Case of Handloom Weavers

In India, the bulk of production activity takes place in the unorganized sector. It is this sector that is likely to absorb increasingly large proportions of the labor force to which the benefits of skill development and the consequent augmentation of productivity should increasingly be extended. At a time when skill development has become a buzzword in the country, we must focus on appropriate skilling for the 86 percent of the working population in the unorganized sector. In a globalizing economy, the Indian workforce, particularly those engaged in the informal sector, will have to contend increasingly with internal and external competition from products and services coming from workers who are relatively better skilled. Mere survival in the market demands retention of one's competitive edge through acquisition of skills and constant upgradation of the skills acquired. The National Sample Survey Office (NSSO)'s 68th-round figures show that among persons of aged 15 years and above, only 2.4 percent had technical degrees or diplomas or certificates. The proportion was 1.1 percent in rural areas and 5.5 percent in urban areas.

The unorganized sector is vast and varied, and the training requirements differ widely across occupations. Although the contribution of this sector toward the gross domestic product (GDP) of the country is about 60 percent, due recognition to the needs of the sector has been slow.

Status of Vocational Training Received/being received per 1,000 population

| Category of person | Receiving formal vocational training | Received vocational training | | | | | | | Did not receive vocational training | Total |
| | | Formal | Hereditary | Nonformal | | | All | | |
				Self-learning	Learning on the job	Others			
1	2	3	4	5	6	7	8	9	10
Rural									
Male	8	16	48	18	42	3	127	864	1,000
Female	3	9	24	13	14	4	64	931	1,000
Person	5	13	37	15	28	4	96	897	1,000
Urban									
Male	19	50	22	28	82	5	186	794	1,000
Female	13	33	9	12	16	6	76	911	1,000
Person	16	42	16	20	50	5	133	850	1,000
Rural + Urban									
Male	11	26	40	21	55	4	146	842	1,000
Female	6	16	20	13	15	4	68	926	1,000
Person	9	22	30	17	35	4	107	884	1,000

Source: National Sample Survey Office (NSSO), *Status of Education and Vocational Training in India, NSS*
Person = Total
68th Round p. 44.

While there is a large (though inadequate) institutional network of training and skill development of workers in the formal sector, facilities in both informal and traditional sectors are grossly inadequate. For instance, surveys show that only about 9 percent of the workforce in small-scale industries are technically trained—most of them only to the Industrial Training Institute (ITI) level. Again, an evaluation of the Prime Minister's Rozgar Yojana conducted by the Institute of Applied Manpower Research (IAMR) in 2000 revealed that more than 50 percent of the applications from potential beneficiaries were rejected on grounds of inadequate skills. The ongoing skill development programs meant for certain specific areas of the informal sector are too disjointed and routine to have a significant impact.

Training and development of jobseekers and workers in the informal sector cannot be easily accommodated within the framework of existing strategies for vocational training. The opportunity cost of training the workers in this sector is high—they cannot afford to forego wages during training. State interventions must address this important area. India will experience economic and skill development challenges in the next two decades. The combined effect of both economic development and skill development has to be fully understood in the overall context of India. There will be four major transformations taking place in the near future according to the survey of Team Lease Services (India Labour Report 2008), as economy will shift from (i) farm to non-farm activities, (ii) rural to urban regions, (iii) unorganized to organized sectors, and (iv) subsistence-oriented self-employment to decent wage employment. All these four transformations will have a direct impact on the skill enhancement of Indian labor force.

Indian government and policymakers at the apex level have responded to the growing challenges of Indian labor force facing the unorganized sector and are trying to give a concrete shape to the policy structure for skill development. Three apex bodies, namely, (i) Prime Minister's National Council on Skill Development, (ii) National Skill Development Coordination Board, and (iii) National Skill Development Corporation are in place and examining various policy options so as to prepare 500 million skilled people by 2022, with a focus on the unorganized sector with sufficient skills to meet the domestic and global requirements.

In this context, the National Policy of Skill Development and Entrepreneurship enshrines the important task of recognizing prior learning (RPL) as the key instrument that can help map the existing skills in the unorganized sector and integrate the informal sector to the formal skilling landscape. The RPL framework is an outcome-based qualification framework linked to National Skills Qualifications Framework (NSQF) against which prior learning through formal/informal channels would be assessed and certified. The RPL process would include a preassessment, skill gap training and final assessment leading to certification of existing skills in an individual. The RPL certification would be at par with the certifications following various skill trainings in the country. It will provide both horizontal and vertical pathways to an individual for acquiring additional skills for better livelihoods. Adequate resources will be earmarked under various government schemes for equitable access to RPL programs. The government will provide detailed guidelines for RPL initiatives that will ensure quality and consistent outcomes.

In this light, an effort is made in this chapter to describe the status of one of the traditional skills predominantly prevalent in the unorganized/informal sector, namely, the handloom industry.

The Handloom Sector—An Overview

The handloom sector is one of the largest unorganized economic activities after agriculture and constitutes an integral part of the rural and semirural livelihood. Handloom weaving constitutes one of the richest and most vibrant aspects of the Indian cultural heritage. The sector has advantages such as being less capital intensive, minimal use of power, being eco-friendly, having flexibility of small production, openness to innovations, and adaptability to market requirements. It is a natural productive asset and tradition at cottage level, which has sustained and grown by transfer of skill from one generation to the next.

Handloom weaving is largely decentralized, and weavers are mainly from the vulnerable and weaker sections of the society, who weave for their household needs and also contribute to the production in the textile sector. The weavers of this industry are keeping alive the traditional craft of different states. The level of artistry and intricacy achieved in the handloom fabrics is unparalleled, and certain weaves/designs are still beyond the scope of modern machines. Handloom sector can meet every need ranging from the exquisite fabrics, which takes months to weave, to popular items of mass production for daily use.

According to the third National Census of Weavers and Allied Workers carried out in 2009 to 2010, more than 4.3 million people are engaged in weaving and allied activities, and the figure was 6.5 million per second handloom census conducted during the period 1995 to 1996.

It is pertinent to highlight some of the major findings of the census.

- Nearly 2.78 million handloom households are engaged in weaving and allied activities, out of which 87 percent are located in rural areas and remaining 13 percent in urban areas.

- The majority (82 percent) of handloom worker households are weaver households, which means at least one member of every such household is engaged in weaving activities. Nearly 14 percent are allied worker households, 3 percent are idle loom households, and about 1 percent are other handloom households having no adult handloom workers.

- In the North-East states, 90 percent of handloom worker households are weaver households. The allied worker households are mostly found in the states outside this region and form 29 percent of the total handloom worker households in these states.

- A caste-wise breakup yields that about 10 percent of handloom worker households belong to the Scheduled Castes (SCs); 22 percent, to Scheduled Tribes (STs); 41 percent, to Other Backward Castes (OBCs); and 27 percent belong to "Other."

- There is a major difference in the caste composition of handloom worker households in the North-East and other states. In the North-East, ST (36 percent) and OBC (33 percent) households have similar proportions of almost a third of the total households, followed by "Other" category households (24 percent), whereas SC households (7 percent) are far less in number. In states outside the North-East, more than half (53 percent) of the handloom worker households are OBCs, followed by households from "Other" (31 percent). SC households account for

14 percent of the total, whereas ST households have a very small presence.

- The caste distribution of handloom weaver households has not undergone any significant changes. In the second handloom census, the OBCs formed the dominant social group, followed by STs and "Other" category households, whereas SC households form the minority group. In the third handloom census too, OBC households formed the majority group and SC households were a minority. There is, however, a slight increase in the "Other" category households accompanied with minor decreases in the proportion of ST and SC households.
- A religion-wise breakup yields that about 78 percent of the households are Hindus, 15 percent Muslims, 6 percent Christians, and the remaining comprising communities such as Buddhists, Sikhs, and others.
- There are differences in the religion-wise composition of handloom worker households in the North-East and other states. In the North-East, 82 percent of the households are Hindus, and 12 percent follow Christianity and other religions. The proportion of Muslim households is small (6 percent). In states outside the North-East, the proportion of Hindu households (70 percent) is comparatively less, and there is a major increase in the proportion of Muslim households (29 percent). Households from other religions account for only 1 percent of the total. Uttar Pradesh (85 percent) and West Bengal (37 percent) emerge as special cases with high proportions of Muslim households.
- Nearly 53 percent of handloom worker households are into commercial production, and nearly 16 percent households undertake a mix of domestic and commercial production. Thus, a total of 69 percent of the handloom households undertake commercial production.
- Nearly 28 percent of handloom worker households are into purely domestic production and mostly located in the North-Eastern states.
- Nearly 3 percent of the handloom households have idle looms and, therefore, no functional handloom worker in the house. Most of such households are in rural areas.

- Nearly 67 percent of households have looms, which may or may not be owned by them. In case of nonownership of looms, the looms are placed in their houses by master weavers, cooperative societies, or private owners. Most (90 percent) households having looms in the house are in rural areas.
- Nearly 33 percent of the handloom worker households do not have looms. These households are either engaged in hired weaving activities, and their members have to go to other locations with looms (like master weaver's premises, cooperative society work sheds, or factories) to do the weaving activity, or these households undertake handloom-allied work. A comparatively higher proportion of households that do not have looms at residence live in urban India.
- At the all-India level, the average annual income of handloom worker households (including those who work only for domestic purpose) is as follows:

Handloom worker households

  ○ Rs.36,498 for total handloom households
  ○ Rs.37,167 for total handloom households residing in rural areas
  ○ Rs.32,030 for total handloom households residing in urban areas,

Weaver households

  ○ Rs.37,707 for total handloom households
  ○ Rs.38,260 for total handloom households residing in rural areas
  ○ Rs.33,038 for total handloom households residing in urban areas.

Allied households

  ○ Rs.29,300 for total handloom households
  ○ Rs.29,693 for total handloom households residing in rural areas
  ○ Rs.26,333 for total handloom households residing in urban areas.

Given the relatively low income levels of handloom-related households in general, many of them suffer from heavy debts, which greatly hampers their capacity to carry on with their profession. In this regard, the census reveals that 0.31 million of handloom households are under debts, and of whom 0.23 million are rural households. Furthermore, it is of interest to know that, for an overwhelming proportion of the households (85.2 percent) the source of loans are private moneylenders, master weavers, and traders, indicating the exploitative financial relations to which the households are subjected. Furthermore, findings reveal that 19.7 percent of households borrowed only for handloom purposes and 7.4 percent borrowed for handloom and other purposes. Also, 27.5 percent of urban households borrowed only for handloom purposes; 10.8 percent of the urban households borrowed for handloom and other purposes; 17.1 percent of rural households borrowed only for handloom purposes; and 6.3 percent of the total households borrowed for handloom and other purposes.

Handlooms: A Dying Industry

A comparison of the weavers enumerated in the second and third census shows a decline in the number of weavers from the second census (3.32 million) to the third (2.99 million), a dissipation of 0.56 million weavers. No doubt, the number of handloom jobs is declining at an alarming rate with a substantial proportion of looms going dysfunctional along with veritable pauperization of weavers and their families. Government's efforts toward reviving handlooms has been a matter of fierce debate among weaver welfare groups and other civic agencies who make fervent demands to protect, promote, and provide sustainable livelihood for those pursuing this traditional occupation. The woes of the poor weavers of handloom industry is depicted in the civic actions of leaders and practitioners of handlooms through hunger strikes and public protests. The following excerpt talks about one such action.

> In 1985, Central government, to ensure that the power-loom did not swallow the handloom completely, made it mandatory for 22 items to be produced only by handloom sector. It included coloured silk cloth, Kanchi silk sarees, dhoti, towel, lungi, hand-kerchiefs. Power-loom mill owners took the issue to the Supreme Court. The Apex Court, in 1986, agreed with the textile policy of the Center, reiterating that the Centre's textile policy was rightly aimed at

giving sufficient work to handloom weavers. Inexplicably the then government reduced these items from 22 to 15. The government in 2008 further reduced it to 11. Never mind, said Prasanna, an activist who was involved for over a decade with Charaka, a handloom initiative. You allow handloom industry to supply the school uniforms to primary and higher secondary school children studying in government schools all over the state, he suggested. The government provided school uniforms free of cost to all its students studying in government schools. Handloom industry spokespersons were saying the same thing over decades, arguing that any such incentives could help the industry survive on its own. The government agreed but a few bureaucrats with the education department found it was a dreary and drudgery life without the incentive they were accustomed to get from the private suppliers of uniforms. Buying from Khadi Gramodyog, under which the handloom sector comes, at best can be account adjustment at the end of the year with no bureaucrat getting any commission. Bureaucrats being evil geniuses found a way out. They delayed the decision to purchase uniforms, then when the schools were about to begin, gave the contract to middlemen to supply to uniforms saying that handloom industry cannot provide such large quantity of supplies in such short period. (https://www.thenewsminute.com/karnatakas/368)

Organizations such as Charaka and its handloom store Desi are midwifing a handloom revival in the country to help the 4.3 million handloom weavers across India. "Everybody knows that if this Handloom Reservation Act is removed, within a year all our handlooms will die," said Prasanna. "That is how handlooms died in the rest of the world. Now 90% of handlooms remain in India and that is because of this Act." (https://scroll.in/article/722078/to-save-handloom-sector-karnatakas-weavers-are-trying-everything-from-padayatras-to-panchayats)

Handloom Weavers in Bangalore

In an effort to have a first-hand knowledge of the living conditions of handloom weavers, the authors had personal meetings with a group of weavers who are presently pursuing their profession in the town of Kanakapura, a small town near Bangalore City, as well as some weavers in Bangalore City. These respondents were identified through Weavers' Service Centre, a Government-of-India initiative, to undertake short-term and observatory training programs in dyeing, printing, designing, and weaving for professionals, students of fashion, textiles, handloom technology, textile designers, dyers, and weavers in the city of Bangalore. In addition, informal enquiries with those in contact with weavers in Kanakapura were used to identify weavers. Informal interviews were carried out with the respondents, using a set of interview guides.

Kanakapura

Kanakapura is a small subdistrict administrative unit belonging to Ramanagara district and is about 70 km from the city of Bangalore. With a population of about 125,000, the town of Kanakapura, a hinterland of Bangalore City, feeds the city with most of the agricultural produce and allied products.

Once a thriving handloom weaving center along with the adjoining town of Anekal, the town had a sizeable population of about 300 handloom weavers. However, sadly, as of today there are only two weavers who are clinging to the traditional handloom weaving, whereas many have taken to power looms. Mr. Nagaraju, a native of the town, said,

> There is no one in the town interested to learn weaving, as there is no income in this profession. Hence, most of the weavers work as laborers or jobs unconnected with handlooms. The sad part is that today's youth here never consider weaving as a livelihood option as they earn higher wages in other unskilled or semiskilled occupations. The garment industry located around Bangalore is a major attraction for these youth who have migrated there.

According to the secretary of Weavers Association at Kanakapura,

> Given the rapid growth of Bangalore City over the past two decades, there are no takers for handlooms and hence they have vanished now. With the death of handloom weaving, the traditional weaving families have now taken to power looms. But power looms too suffer from

sever power shortage. Moreover, skilled weavers are diminishing day by day. So we have labor issues that have affected production.

Typically, weavers get orders for sarees from "master weavers" located in Bangalore, who also provide the required yarn as well as design with a stipulated number of finished product. The weaver makes the products and supplies them to the master weaver on a predetermined price, almost always to the advantage of the latter. It was reported that a hired weaver is paid Rs.110 per saree, and he or she can weave a maximum of two sarees in a day provided there is uninterrupted power. The master weaver sells the products to businesses dealing with sarees at a premium and earns profit.

Our respondent further said that there are 15 weaver families who have 15 to 20 looms and supply their products to wholesale dealers elsewhere. However, a majority have only 2 to 5 looms. Presently, there are 300 members registered in the Weavers Association. Interestingly, many weavers work in different occupations during the daytime and resume to weaving activities in the evening to supplement their incomes. Furthermore, 8 to 10 families have rented out their looms to laborers on a rental of Rs.2,000 per month. More and more families are resorting to this nowadays. Modernization of power looms is slowly picking up here for those who can make bigger investments. The advantages of computer technology in this sector are reduced work time, increased production, and better quality of products. In addition, system can be operated by anyone with minimum education. However, upgrading to this technology would require a minimum investment of Rs.400,000, which is beyond the investment capacity of most of the weaver households. Given this, most of the children of weaver families have either gone out for education or work as autorikshaw (the ubiquitous three-wheeler taxi) drivers or take up other odd jobs in Bangalore City, as they do not prefer to stay in the town.

Many of the respondents who spoke with us said that focused priority needs to be given to establish textile parks where adequate infrastructure for weavers must be made available. Furthermore, most of the financial assistance through loans and subsidies do not reach the intended poor beneficiaries due to delays, complicated procedures, and corruption. So much so, these benefits are garnered by those who are financially powerful and exert political influence.

Weavers of Yelahanka

The second set of weavers contacted live in Yelahanka, a small township and a part of the Bangalore City. The meeting was organized by the Weavers' Service Centre, a Government-of-India initiative, to undertake short-term and observatory training programs in dyeing, printing, designing, and weaving for professionals, students of fashion, textile, handloom technology, textile designers, dyers, and weavers in the city of Bangalore. Within the town of Yelahanka there are four layouts where weavers function in small bylanes in a dingy environment. The weaver layouts is best described by Devki Pande:

> Yelahanka is a green suburb of Bangalore. Ideal to live in, ideal to study in—so people say. They don't mention the power cuts, or that there are precisely two affordable places to eat in. They don't mention that the closest shopping arena is an hour away. But instead of a panoramic viewpoint, let us focus instead on the linear settlement parallel to the Yeswanthpuram Railway tracks. It has been building up for ages now; generations of people from Andhra Pradesh have fled to Bangalore because of the lack of availability of jobs back in their hometown. Or that's what they say. Running is such a commonplace activity, so much so that what does it matter if they are running towards a better life, or running away from persecution? Within the community from Andhra is a smaller subset of people who weave with silk and cotton and jute, transforming them from raw fibers to threads, and then saris of exquisite detail—and it only boosts the economy of Yelahanka.
>
> They have converted the bright orange, neon green, and blue (a blue that matches the concave of the sky) houses into their little factories. The factories are not compatible with the steel-stained, marble-floored, smoke-puffing images; instead of open spaces there are corridors so thin that just a single person can venture forth at a time, openings on the sides, rickety staircases that creak with every footstep, shaking a shower of spiders and cobwebs on the already dusty ground, and more corridors and enclosures—where looms are housed. The click-clack of the looms is a common sound to hear around that area, even comforting, because it is a sign of life in a deserted community of a deserted suburb. Shops and auto-stands have sprung up around these

weavers; carts of coconut sellers with coconuts ranging from palm green to olive green, ready to engage in a tongue-clacking bargaining session. Occasionally a train ambles past, screeches, or tries to, to a halt, and travels about a hundred meters before it complies with the dictionary definition of stopping. (https://devkipande.wordpress .com/2014/10/13/weavers-of-yelahanka/)

At the Weavers Service Center, we were met by six weavers who operated in Yelahanka. The major problems faced by these weavers is summarized as follows:

- No professional weavers are available now even if we want to employ. Most of the weavers have abandoned their profession and are taking up other jobs such as security guards and so on, which give them some assured income.
- For those in business, the price of silk yarn is skyrocketing every day and, hence, not affordable to most of the weavers.
- Very poor marketing support for products. Weavers are unable to bargain for viable rates with the businessmen who coerce weavers to sell at cost price, or at power loom rates, which is a huge loss.
- Earlier the entire family was engaged in all the weaving-related activities. Now women and children go away seeking work outside for wages.
- The competition is so aggressive that only big players with high investments and big business network will thrive while the poor weavers are at the mercy of the former.
- Currently, the weavers hired as wage laborer earn Rs.250 per day. Most respondents urged that the wages must be at least Rs.600 per day for a decent living.
- It was suggested that to achieve stabilization of selling rates the government's Handloom Development Corporation must take the responsibility of supplying pure yarns at reasonable, affordable rates.
- While there is a Silk Exchange for the benefit of silk reelers, there is none for weavers. This is a major lacuna, and establishment of such an agency would go a long way in addressing the problems of marketing of weavers' products.

- The newly introduced Goods and Services Tax (GST) by the government has added to the misery of weaver businessmen due to complicated procedures of filing frequent returns, new accounting procedures, and timely compliance norms. This is so as most of the weavers are illiterate or semiliterates and not conversant with various procedures. The weavers were unanimous in demanding a total exemption of GST for all handloom products.

- Handloom industry is no longer attractive as a viable profession to lead a dignified living due to poor wages and harsh working conditions. This has deterred most of the youth in weaver families to look out for other occupations.

- However, there is a need for protecting the interests of existing handloom weavers who are totally bereft of many facilities that would work as incentives. The role of government in providing relief to this community needs no overemphasis.

- On its part, the government must introduce medical insurance for weavers, as most of them are past their middle age.

- There is need for setting up a death relief fund that ensures a minimum of Rs.150,000 to the next of kin whenever a weaver dies.

- As weavers work in dark small houses, uninterrupted power supply at the looms is a requisite that must be provided free of cost.

- There is an urgent need to establish handloom technology development institutions to update and introduce latest developments in the industry that would offer opportunities for successful careers to young aspirants.

- There is an urgent need for providing exposure to weavers by organizing tours to successful cooperatives and weaver collectives in other states.

- All the respondents said that the government must build a mechanism to purchase and supply silk yarn to save the handloom sector.

It is clear that handloom industry and a large group of handloom weavers face severe hardships to pursue their profession for a variety of reasons, notwithstanding several governmental efforts to uplift them through several schemes. The avowed goal of the National Policy of Skill Development to recognize prior learning of a multitude of traditional skill workers, artisans, and crafts persons is expected to provide succor.

CHAPTER 5

Conclusions

The vocational education system in India faces a daunting task in achieving the ambitious goals of National Skill Development and Entrepreneurship policy of 2015. Foremost, the vocational education stream itself has poor visibility due to several reasons, like low awareness among stakeholders and lack of parity in wage structure between formally qualified and vocationally trained graduates. Furthermore, public perception on skilling—that it is the last option for those who have not been able to progress/opted out of the formal academic system—is also a reason for the low demand for vocational education. This is due mainly to the tendency of industry to discriminate skilled and unskilled persons, depriving the skilled workforce of any meaningful economic incentive. This is also compounded by the fact that most of the vocational training programs are not aligned to the requirements of the industry. Vocational education and training is a function of skill development. However, there has not been a well-crafted, exclusive vocational education policy focusing on the contemporary industrial needs of the country.

Potentially, the target group for skill development comprises all those in the labor force, including those entering the labor market for the first time (12.8 million annually), those employed in the organized sector (26.0 million), and those working in the unorganized sector (433 million) in 2004 to 2005. The very fact that a huge proportion of skilled labor is in the unorganized sector poses a veritable challenge. Furthermore, leveraging a huge "demographic dividend" of more than 62 percent of its population in the working-age group (15 to 59 years) and over 54 percent of its total population below 25 years of age is easier said than done. Major reasons in this regard include (a) poor level of skills possessed by the vast majority of those joining the workforce due to high rates of school dropouts; (b) inadequate skills training capacity; (c) a negative perception around skilling; and (d) low employability of even those holding professional qualifications, such as degrees in different engineering disciplines. Overarching these factors, and as an effect, is the low priority given to accomplishing high *quality* among the skilled workforce.

The newly created Ministry of Skill Development and Entrepreneurship mentions clearly in its policy framework that skilling will be integrated with formal education by introducing vocational training classes linked to the local economy from class 9 onwards in at least 25 percent of the schools, over the next 5 years. Seamless integration of vocational training in formal education is expected to ignite student interest.

The industrial and labor market trends clearly indicate the necessity of strengthening vocational education in India on a priority basis. The introduction of vocational education at secondary level through bivalent schools will help broaden the vocational education base at secondary level of education and help create potential skilled workforce. Framing of vocational qualification framework, introduction of vocational degrees, and setting up of a vocational university with polytechnics, community colleges, community polytechnics, and other vocational education programs, such as affiliated colleges, are some of the recommendations that require further deliberation. The poignant goal of the present government, "Make in India" (which includes major new initiatives designed to facilitate investment, foster innovation, protect intellectual property, and build best-in-class manufacturing infrastructure), further necessitates the revamping of education system through institutionalizing professionally planned skill development education programs where quality and competitiveness form critical guiding forces.

There is a mismatch between what is demanded by industry and the types of skills supplied. Addressing this dichotomy would pave the way for addressing quality issues. Sharing experiences will be increasingly important, which would enable India to access experiences of other Asian countries, identifying and adopting best practices as well as building effective and implementable strategies to address challenges. Furthermore, proactive international partnerships in skill development programs would go a long way in enhancing the quality of programs as well as finding effective pathways for promoting professionalism among the skilled workforce.

In an internationally competitive training environment, the implementation of quality management systems in vocational education and training (VET) can provide a competitive advantage in preparing the quality workforce required for micro- and macro-economic reforms. It is imperative that quality of inputs provided to students must be of high caliber—implying the adoption of a quality management system. As mentioned elsewhere, studies indicate that there is a lack of emphasis on quality in training transaction, curriculum, training infrastructure, and a host of other aspects. The challenge is to facilitate these institutions to keep pace with the fast-growing technological demands for industry and the expanding universe of knowledge through a well-designed quality paradigm. Furthermore, such an attempt to enhance the quality of training and training infrastructure through improved design and delivery system would, more importantly, have positive employment outcomes of graduates from the vocational training system, especially in the existing industrial and economic scenarios where considerably high demand for professional technicians exist. Currently, different norms and parameters apply across different skill development schemes, thus making implementation very challenging for training providers and states.

Nevertheless, it must be mentioned that serious efforts are being made to address the "quality" issue. The opportunities in this respect are several. As part of its "mandate" National Skill Development Corporation is working on designing the standards for skill development in India. The National Occupational Standards (NOS) specify the standard of performance that an individual must achieve when carrying out a function in the workplace, together with the knowledge and understanding they need to meet a standard consistently. The NOS are laid down by the Sector Skill Councils (SSCs) with the participation of the industry. A set of NOS, aligned to a job role, called Qualification Pack (QP), would be available for every job role in each industry sector. These drive both the creation of curriculum and the assessment of performance. Thus, NSQF will make it possible to drive competency-based training for every job role in industry that will help to meet all the quality challenges in terms of training. The SSCs are also required to update or upgrade the NOS and QPs as per the advancement of time and technology. Currently, there are 1661 QPs covering 4,420 unique NOS across 32 sectors.

Including women in our productive workforce is critical for the economic development of India. As per a study by the International Monetary Fund (IMF), India's gross domestic product (GDP) can expand by a huge 27 percent if the number of women workers increases to the same level as that of men (Economic Times 2015). The skill initiatives have focused on this, and some of the large schemes such as Standard Training Assessment and Reward (STAR) and Pradhan Mantri Kaushal Vikas Yojana (PMKVY) have achieved close to 40 percent women participation, which is considered to be a significant achievement.

A well-crafted training programs for developing entrepreneurial skills is an important element of skill development. This is clearly enunciated in the National Policy of Skill Development. Vibrant entrepreneurship requires support from an enabling ecosystem of culture, finance, expertise, infrastructure, skills, and business-friendly regulations. Many government and nongovernment organizations are playing enabling roles across each of these crucial supporting elements.

Being a vast nation with physical and sociocultural diversities with a significant proportion of population being poor and less literate, India desperately needs to adopt an inclusive philosophy and policy where the poor and the disadvantaged are given prominence. A case in point is that of handloom weavers whose age-old profession is fast-dying due to a variety of factors. Like handloom weavers, there are many other traditional rural artisans who contribute significantly to the nation's growth but are living in utter poverty and despair. The National Skills Policy indeed has recognized the need to protect these sections through recognition of prior learning and initiate appropriate steps to protect, promote, and wherever possible, upscale their skills. It is true that given the vastness and diversities of India, this is indeed a veritable challenge. However, if there is strong administrative will and political determination, this challenge is not insurmountable and can be overcome.

References

Asian Development Bank. 2006. *Financing Technical Vocational Education and Training in the People's Republic of China*. Manila: Asian Development Bank (Technical Assistance 4868-PRC).

Asia-Pacific Economic Cooperation (APEC). 2013. *A Report on the APEC Region Labour Market: Evidence of Skills Shortages and General Trends in Employment and the Value of Better Labour Market Information Systems*. Singapore: APEC Human Resources Development Working Group.

Chenoy, D. December, 2012. *Skill Development in India, A Transformation in the Making*. Mumbai, India: IDFC.

Dhar, A. August 15, 2016. "Skills Development in a Global Context: Towards a Future Ready Workforce, Inauguration of first Human Capital Summit, Colombo, Srilanka." *The World Bank*. http://www.worldbank.org/en/news/speech/2016/08/15/skills-development-in-a-global-context-towards-a-future-ready-workforce

Emerging Markets Consulting. 2014. "Survey of ASEAN Employers on Skills and Competitiveness." ILO Asia Pacific Working Paper Series, Bangkok.

Federation of Indian Chambers of Commerce and Industry. 2006. *FICCI Survey on "The state of Industrial Training Institutes in India."* New Delhi: FICCI.

Freeman, R. 2006. *The Great Doubling: The Challenge of the New Global Labor Market*. 2006 Unpublished. http://emlab.berkeley.edu/users/webfac/eichengreen/e183_sp07/great_doub.pdf

Galvão, M.E. 2014. *Making the Case for Vocational Education and Training Improvement: Issues and Challenges*. Turin, Italy: European Training Foundation.

Gandhi, M. K. July 31, 1937. *Harijan*. Ahmedabad: Navajivan Publishing House.

Gasskov, V. 2000. Managing Vocational Training Systems: Handbook for Senior Administrators. Geneva: ILO.

Government of India, *Ministry of Skill Development & Entrepreneurship, Annual Report 2016-17)*

Government of India, Planning Commission. 2013. Planning Commission 2013. http://planningcommission.nic.in/hackathon/Skill%20Development.pdf

Government of India, *Scheme of Community Development through Polytechnics-Norms & Guidelines*, Department of Higher Education Ministry of Human Resource Development Government of India New Delhi February, 2009.

Government of India. 2015. "The National Policy for Skill Development and Entrepreneurship 2015." http://www.skilldevelopment.gov.in/National-Policy-2015.html

International Labour Organization. 2003. *Industrial Training Institutes of India: The efficiency study report*. Geneva: ILO.http://voced.edu.au/content/ngv1141

India Labour Report. 2008. "A report by TeamLease Services." http://www.team-lease.com/sites/default/files/resources/teamlease_labourreport2008.pdf

Joshi, S., G. Pandey, and B.K. Sahoo. 2014. "Comparing Public and Private Vocational Training Providers." In *India's Skills Challenge: Reforming Vocational Education and Training to Harness the Demographic Dividend*, edited by S. Mehrotra, 86-128. New Delhi: Oxford University Press.

Martinez-Fernandez, C., and M. Powell. 2009. *Employment and Skills Strategies in Southeast Asia Setting the Scene*. Paris, France: OECD.

Mehrotra, S. 2014a. From 5 to 20 million a year: The challenge of scale, quality and relevance in India's TVET. *Prospects* 44, no. 2, pp. 267–277. http://link.springer.com/article/10.1007%2Fs11125-014-9305-2

Mehrotra, S. (ed.). 2014b. *India's Skills Challenge: Reforming Vocational Education and Training to Harness the Demographic Dividend*. Oxford University Press. https://thewire.in/110808/skills-development-budget-government

Mehrotra, S., A. Gandhi, B.K. Sahoo, and P. Saha. 2012. *Creating Employment in the 12th Five Year Plan*. Institute of Applied Manpower Research (IAMR Occasional Paper No.3/2012) Planning Commission, Government of India, May, 2012.

National Sample Survey Office (NSSO). *Status of Education and Vocational Training in India, NSS 68th Round p.44*

National Skill Development Corporation. n.d. *Need Assessment Report on Building Trainers' Skills in Vocational Employability*. New Delhi: NSDC.

Nayak, A. K., and V. K. Rao. 2008. *Secondary Education*, 147. New Delhi, India: APH Publishing.

Panth, B. 2013. "Skills Training and Workforce Development with Reference to Underemployment and Migration." In *Skills Development for Inclusive and Sustainable Growth in Developing Asia-Pacific. Volume 19 of Technical and Vocational Education and Training: Issues, Concerns and Prospects*, eds. R. Maclean, S. Jagannathan, and J. Sarvi, (pp. 195–212). Dordrecht, Netherlands: Springer.

Pilz, M., and S. Wilmshöfer. 2015. "The Challenges of Formal, Non-formal and Informal Learning in Rural INDIA: The Case of Fishing Families on the Chilika Lagoon, Orissa." *Prospects* 45, no. 2, pp. 231–243.

Pilz, M., and J. Li. 2014. Tracing Teutonic footprints in VET around the world? The skills development strategies of German companies in the USA, China and India. *European Journal of Training and Development* 38, no. 8, pp. 745–763.

Planning Commission. n.d. *The Impact and Prospects of the Community College System in India*, Socioeconomic Research Division, Planning Commission,

Government of India 2003. http://planningcommission.gov.in/reports/sereport/ser/stdy_commty.pdf

Planning Commission. 2003. *The Impact and Prospects of the Community College System in India*. Socioeconomic Research Division, Planning Commission, Government of India. http://planningcommission.gov.in/reports/sereport/ser/stdy_commty.pdf

Rao, K. S., B. K. Sahoo, and D. Ghosh. 2014. "The Indian Vocational Education and Training System: An Overview." In *India's Skills Challenge: Reforming Vocational Education and Training to Harness the Demographic Dividend*, edited by S. Mehrotra, 37–85. New Delhi: Oxford University Press.

Ra, S., C. Brian, and A. Liu. 2015. *Challenges and Opportunities for Skills Development in Asia Changing Supply, Demand, and Mismatches*. Manila: Asian Development Bank.

Singh, M. 2012. "India's National Skill Development Policy and Implications for TVET and Lifelong Learning." In *The Future of Vocational Education and Training in a Changing World*, edited by M. Pilz, 179-211. Wiesbaden: Springer VS.

Sungsup Ra, B. Chin, and A. Liu. 2015. *Challenges And Opportunities For Skills Development In Asia Changing Supply, Demand, And Mismatches*. Mandaluyong, Philippines: Asian Development Bank.

Sykes, M. 1988. *The Story Of Nai Talim: Fifty Years Of Education At Sevagrram India (1937-1987)*. Willowbrook, IL: The Swaraj Foundation

Tara, N., and M.V. Kumar. n.d. "Skill Development." (unpublished)

The Economic Times. September 6, 2015. "Gender parity in workforce can boost India's GDP by 27%: Christine Lagarde." https://economictimes.indiatimes.com/news/economy/indicators/gender-parity-in-workforce-can-boost-indias-gdp-by-27-christine-lagarde/articleshow/48847069.cms

UNESCO and UNICEF. 2013. *Asia-Pacific End of Decade Notes on Education for All: Universal Primary Education*. Bangkok: UNESCO and UNICEF.

World *Bank*. 2012. *More and Better Jobs in South Asia*. Washington, DC: World Bank.

Web links

http://ficci.in/spdocument/20073/imacs.pdf

http://handlooms.nic.in/Writereaddata/Handloom%20report.pdf

http://jaypanda.in/wp-content/uploads/2017/05/ITIs.pdf

http://mospi.nic.in/sites/default/files/publication_reports/nss_report_no_566_21sep15_0.pdf

http://planningcommission.gov.in/plans/planrel/fiveyr/2nd/2planch23.html

http://planningcommission.gov.in/reports/sereport/ser/stdy_commty.pdf

http://shodhganga.inflibnet.ac.in/bitstream/10603/7053/7/07_chapter%202.pdf

http://shodhganga.inflibnet.ac.in/bitstream/10603/7053/8/08_chapter%203.pdf

http://www.domain-b.com/economy/budget/union_budget_2017

http://www.etf.europa.eu/webatt.nsf/0/270970490A6E9327C1257CA8004070
    38/$file/Quality%20assurance%20in%20VET.pdf

http://www.mkgandhi.org/articles/basic_edu.htm

http://www.swaraj.org/shikshantar/naitalimmarjoriesykes.htm

http://www.tvet-online.asia/issue7/tara_etal_tvet7.pdf

http://www.vkmaheshwari.com/WP/?p=1389

http://www.worldbank.org/en/news/speech/2016/08/15/skills-development-
    in-a-global-context-towards-a-future-ready-workforce

http://www.worldbank.org/en/news/speech/2016/08/15/skills-development-
    in-a-global-context-towards-a-future-ready-workforce

https://scroll.in/article/722078/to-save-handloom-sector-karnatakas-weavers-
    are-trying-everything-from-padayatras-to-panchayats

https://www.oecd.org/employment/leed/45592893.pdf

https://www.oecd.org/g20/summits/toronto/G20-Skills-Strategy.pdf

https://www.thenewsminute.com/karnatakas/368

www.ficci.in/spdocument/20405/FICCI-KPMG-Global-Skills-report.pdf

www.unevoc.unesco.org/up/India_Country_Paper.pdf

Suggested Readings

Chandra, R. 2003. *Encyclopedia of Education in South Asia.* Vol. 2, 117–118. New Delhi, India: Kalpaz Publications.

Federation of Indian Chamber of Commerce and Industry-KPMG. n.d. "Skilling India—A look back at the Progress, Challenges and the Way Forward." ficci.in/spdocument/20405/FICCI-KPMG-Global-Skills-report.pdf

Federation of Indian Chamber of Commerce and Industry (FICCI). 2010. *Skill Development Landscape in India and Implementing Quality Skills Training.* ICRA Management Consulting Services Limited.

Federation of Indian Chamber of Commerce and Industry (FICCI)-KPMG,

International Labour Office. 2014. *Survey of ASEAN Employers on Skills and Competitiveness.* Bangkok: ILO.

International Labour Office. 2010. *A Skilled Workforce for Strong, Sustainable and Balanced Growth A G20 Training Strategy.* Geneva, Switzerland: ILO.

Lall, S. 1999. *Competing with Labour: Skills and Competitiveness in Developing Countries.* Geneva: ILO. http://www.ilo.org/employment/Whatwedo/Publications/WCMS_123613/lang--en/index.htm

Narayan, S. 1968. *The Selected Works of Mahatma Gandhi* (6 Volumes). Ahmedabad, India: Navajivan Publishing House.

Tara, N., N. S. Kumar, and M. Pilz. 2016. "Quality of VET in India: The case of Industrial Training Institutes." In: TVET@Asia, no. 7, pp. 1–17. http://www.tvet-online.asia/issue7/tara_etal_tvet7.pdf

UNESCO Institute for Statistics. 2012. *Adult and Youth Literacy. UIS Fact Sheet September 2012, No. 20.* Montreal: UNESCO.

UNEVOC-UNESCO. n.d. *Dr. Vijay P. Goel, Technical and Vocational Education and Training (TVET) system in India for Sustainable Development*

World Bank. 2013. World Development Report 2013: Jobs. Washington, DC.

World Bank. January, 2008. *Skill Development in India—The Vocational Education and Training System, Report No.22, South Asia Human Development Sector.* Washington, DC: World Bank.

Index

OTHER TITLES IN THE HUMAN RESOURCE MANAGEMENT AND ORGANIZATIONAL BEHAVIOR COLLECTION

- *Practical Performance Improvement: How to Be an Exceptional People Manager* by Rod Matthews
- *Creating Leadership: How to Change Hippos Into Gazelles* by Philip Goodwin and Tony Page
- *Conflict and Leadership: How to Harness the Power of Conflict to Create Better Leaders and Build Thriving Teams* by Christian Muntean
- *Precision Recruitment Skills: How to Find the Right Person For the Right Job, the First Time* by Rod Matthews
- *Managing Organizational Change: The Measurable Benefits of Applied iOCM* by Linda C. Mattingly
- *Creating the Accountability Culture: The Science of Life Changing Leadership* by Yvonnne Thompson
- *The HOW of Leadership: Inspire People to Achieve Extraordinary Results* by Maxwell Ubah
- *Lead Self First Before Leading Others: A Life Planning Resource* by Stephen K. Hacker and Marvin Washington
- *The Concise Coaching Handbook: How to Coach Yourself and Others to Get Business Results* by Elizabeth Dickinson
- *Leading the High-Performing Company: A Transformational Guide to Growing Your Business and Outperforming Your Competition* by Heidi Pozzo
- *How Successful Engineers Become Great Business Leaders* by Paul Rulkens
- *Creating a Successful Consulting Practice* by Gary W. Randazzo

Announcing the Business Expert Press Digital Library

Concise e-books business students need for classroom and research

This book can also be purchased in an e-book collection by your library as

- *a one-time purchase,*
- *that is owned forever,*
- *allows for simultaneous readers,*
- *has no restrictions on printing, and*
- *can be downloaded as PDFs from within the library community.*

Our digital library collections are a great solution to beat the rising cost of textbooks. E-books can be loaded into their course management systems or onto students' e-book readers. The **Business Expert Press** digital libraries are very affordable, with no obligation to buy in future years. For more information, please visit **www.businessexpertpress.com/librarians**. To set up a trial in the United States, please email **sales@businessexpertpress.com**.